What Are People Saying About This Book?

Over the past twenty years we have seen the consistent passion that Ron and Tina have for healthy marriages and families. They live it, they fight for it and they have a very unique gift to bring restoration and healing to the most challenging cases. We have recommended their ministry to various couples with amazing breakthrough results.

David and Cheryl Koop
Coastal Church, Vancouver, BC

"I told Gene, I'm willing to have a relationship with you but not this one–so he agreed to work on it. We were recommended to the Couples Retreat by our staff. Gene was reluctant to go at first but once he was there he realized that if he didn't complete the Relationship Lifeline that I wasn't going to stay with him and the children were on board with me as they were off to college.

I believe once you have decided to have children, you've decided to make a commitment for the rest of your life and that's a commitment that is unwavering. I knew once I had children there were sacrifices I had to make. I was willing and able."

Shannon Tweed Simmons
Actress (Wife of Gene Simmons – KISS)

Ron and Tina Konkin, all I can say is that is what God is doing in their ministry...has been a 100% success! I get emails all the time saying, that their marriage is saved – because of Relationship Lifeline.

Matthew Cork,
Yorba Linda Friends Church , Yorba Linda, CA

As a pastor I face the never ending saga of marriages in crisis. I have found that marriage problems can be one of the most painful and disruptive issues of life. I believe every marriage can be saved but it takes true honesty and vulnerability. Ron and Tina have the ability to help couples get past the surface issues and right to the root of the pain. I have had them minister in my church and watched them have a dramatic impact on my people. I would strongly recommend them to anyone or any church as not only engaging speakers but also speakers that are desperately needed in our culture.

Pastor Gary Keesee
Faith Life Church, Johnstown, OH

Ron and Tina Konkin go where angels fear to tread. Their relationship seminars are truly revolutionary and go straight to the heart of the matter. Change your heart and you will change your life. The truth sets people free.

Keith and Mary Hudson *(www.keithhudson.org)*
Evangelists (Katy Perry's Parents)

"We entered the weekend rather reluctantly, simply expecting to experience just 'another' marriage seminar. What happened in those few days was more than an experience; it was an encounter that rocked our marriage! We experienced lasting transformation in such a deep level, that the only word that can describe it is - miraculous! Ron and Tina Konkin are not only truly gifted- they are a true gift to everyone's marriage!"

Anthony & Madeleine Greco,
Pastors, Calgary Life Church

Ron and Tina Konkin are marriage miracle workers. After sending countless couples through their program we can truly say God has anointed this ministry. Ron and Tina are relevant and real. Their resources and techniques touch your soul and equip you to take proactive steps in your future.

As pastors for 35 years we have finally found a marriage program that works. We are confident to entrust our friends, family and congregation to the Relationship Lifeline.

Pastor Phil and Tammy Hotsenpiller
Influence Church, Anaheim Hills, CA

"I have known Ron and Tina Konkin for over 30 years and observed one overwhelming fact - their success and longevity in Teaching is due to their love for people which created in them a great desire to see people made whole. To say they have done a good job at it is an understatement to say the least."

Don McMillan
Pastor

"Whether your relationship is in crisis, or it is stagnant and you are looking to break some unhealthy patterns or behaviors of the past, or you are in "a good place" but yearn to dig deeper and explore the possibilities of your relationships potential... Tina and Ron Konkin's Relationship Lifeline is remarkable!!

We know... we were there.

We went in looking to dig deeper and take our communication, respect, and love for one another to new heights.

We wanted to find out how. We wanted to see if it was possible.

We were slightly incredulous at first but Tina and Ron's process peeled away the layers (and years) of resentment, bad habits, complacency, and miscommunication and replaced that with renewed passion, respect, gratitude, and understanding.

We were stunned. We highly recommend it for any couple that is in a crisis, wants to break the chains of complacency, or want to explore the possibilities of taking their relationship to heights only previously dreamed possible."

Chynna Phillips & Billy Baldwin
Singer (Wilson Phillips) & Actor

L VE
SEX & MONEY

The R3 Factor
of Great Relationships

Ron & Tina Konkin

emerge
publishing

TULSA, OKLAHOMA

22 21 20 19 18 17   8 7 6 5 4 3 2

LOVE, SEX AND MONEY–The R3 Factor for Great Relationships

emerge
publishing
TULSA, OKLAHOMA

Published by:
Emerge Publishing, LLC
9521B Riverside Parkway, Suite 243
Tulsa, Oklahoma 74137
Phone: 888.407.4447
www.EmergePublishing.com

Library of Congress Cataloging-in-Publication Data

ISBN: 978-1-943127-55-9 Paperback
ISBN: 978-1-943127-56-6 Digital/E-book

BISAC Category:
FAM013000 FAMILY & RELATIONSHIPS / Conflict Resolution
FAM030000 FAMILY & RELATIONSHIPS / Marriage & Long-Term Relationships

Printed in the United States of America.

TABLE OF CONTENTS

PART 2: MONEY SECTION

DEDICATION

To our daughter Mia.

Thank you for reminding us that life is made up of 30-second miracles. You are one of them!

Mom & Dad

About the Authors

Tina Konkin

Tina was born in Liege, Belgium and immigrated to the small town of Thompson, Manitoba when she was 8 years old. Tina is no stranger to family dysfunction. She was the victim of sexual and physical abuse. She was also bullied in school as a child, because she was an immigrant and couldn't speak English. Tina's amazing story of survival and strength is inspiring. Today she realizes that her hardships do not define her. Instead, they are pages to her life story. It's a story that she shares to bring hope and healing to others.

In Memory of
Ron Konkin

Ron was originally from a small town of Fruitvale, BC and moved to Vancouver, when he got married to Tina. Growing up in a home with 16 foster children caused Ron to experience real hurt, heartaches and grief that resulted from broken families.

On December 25, 2013, surrounded by his family, Ronald Alan Konkin passed away on Christmas morning after his four year journey with cancer.

Ron had true compassion for people and his dream was to see families restored. As founder of Relationship Lifeline, he influenced and played a key role in the healing of many lives, marriages and families. His hope when you read this book, was for you to be inspired to find healing in all areas of your life and to enable you to have healthy relationships and families.

Ron is survived by Tina Konkin, his wife of 32 years and his 3 children, Jenny Michelle, Joshua John, Mia Ream, Mary Hudson (daughter in law) and 2 grandchildren, Scarlett and Hudson.

INTRODUCTION

"…when emotions run high, intelligence runs low." Kerry Patterson

–Ron

This book is not just another world-view about LOVE, SEX and MONEY, but rather a personal journey of how these three areas affect you and your relationships. Any one of the three independently—LOVE, SEX or MONEY—can make or break a relationship.

If we asked you to tell us about the relationship of your dreams, would it be close to your reality? Are you disappointed that no matter how hard you try you can't make it happen? What clouds the expanse between here and there?

Is your reality a space filled with pain, tension, arguments and distance between the one you want more than anything to be close to? Does each fight intensify to the point where you don't even remember what you were arguing about?

Relationship—despite our best intentions—is difficult, and yet we crave the very connection we inadvertently destroy.

How do you know you are operating in LOVE and not in damaged love? Do you even know what love is? Has physical touch and SEX been emulated in a healthy way as you grew up? What were you taught about MONEY?

In the 20 years of working with relationships, I have yet to meet someone that has mastered all three areas. The reason for that is because they are not constant. Each one of these topics in itself has filled volumes of books by experts trying to give us the best strategies and plans in how not to fail in these areas of relationship. The problem is, as our relationships grow and hopefully mature, they keep changing their faces and we are in constant flux as to how to change along with them.

In this book, we want to give you the tools you need to understand and identify what is working and, conversely, not working for you in your relationships—with yourself, others and spiritually.

Many of us are looking for a magic formula we can pull out of our pocket in difficult situations. We want an easy fix with a favorable end result. In fact, if we're honest, we believe good relationships should just happen. We all just want to get along and be happy.

But it's not that easy, is it?

Happiness evades us and the relationship slowly—one misunderstanding at a time—deteriorates into a shell of what it once was. If only there was a "formula" we could use to get to the root of the issue so we could see beyond the clutter in our relationships.

Dear Reader, it is our hope as relationship experts to offer you a simple solution to help you find not a formula but true healing as thousands of others have discovered who dared to adopt the R3 FACTOR into their lives.

The R3 FACTOR of great relationships involves revealing our present reality, rewriting that reality and renewing to create a new reality.

The healing process we want to introduce to you is both simple and yet profound, and it will change your relationships.

Tina and I hope you will seize this moment and fight for the love you deserve, the intimacy within you, and the financial freedom you have always dreamed of.

In this book, we delve into these three realms in great detail. Our hope is that this book will transform your relational life—both personally and in ALL of your relationships.

<u>The R3 Factor</u>

1. Reveal - Yesterday

2. Rewrite - Today

3. Renew - Tomorrow

CHAPTER 1

THE DEMISE OF RELATIONSHIP

"The family is both the fundamental unit of society as well as the root of culture. It…is a perpetual source of encouragement, advocacy, assurance, and emotional refueling that empowers a child to venture with confidence into the greater world and to become all that he can be." – Marianne E. Neifert

–Ron

Today, more so than in any generation, we suffer from an instant gratification epidemic.

It is a disease that has gone rampant and spread over the globe. Children and relationships, more than anything else, suffer because of it. Our relationships become shallow and easily disposed. The motto seems to be, "If it doesn't feel good, move on" or "This just isn't working for me anymore" or "It isn't you, it's just me," etc.

Our concern in Orange County, California, where Tina and I reside, is the divorce rate for a first-time marriage is a whopping 72%. Sadly in many of these divorces or separations children are the victims.

In over twenty years of experience answering 911 relationship crisis calls, Tina and I have found ourselves as acting relational trauma physicians. Dealing with the excruciating pain of watching families fall apart over and over again, lit a passion in us for individuals, couples and families who need true healing; not just temporary pain relief. To help the hurting move past the immediate breakdown or crisis at hand, we needed to refocus them and challenge them to see the real problem or the true issues—not just where to assign blame for their current melt down.

Tina and I are honored and humbled when we consider that God chose us to do this work. The success rate is over 90% for couples who are already separated or filing for divorce who have attended the intensive weekends we offer!

We began to analyze what we were offering in the seminars to produce such significant change and lasting results. We both knew our limitations and abilities, but we also understood, as Christian believers, that God has laws in operation. Simply put, the law of gravity states that whatever goes up will come down. And whether you are a believer or not, it is an established law God has set from the beginning of time. It is a certifiable truth.

We began to suspect we had tapped into some relational laws, one of which is what goes in will come out. Based on the results we asked ourselves a couple of pertinent questions: What do we do and how do we do it to beat such incredible odds?

The question remained, why do we have such a high success rate. All of a sudden, our formula or law of the

R3 FACTOR; REVEAL, REWRITE, and RENEW made complete and utter sense.

What do we do? Part one of the R3 FACTOR is teaching people the importance of the REVEAL process. Dr. Phil McGraw, coined the now popular phrase, "You can't change or heal what you don't acknowledge". Today, we are hearing more and more about the importance of our personal story and how significant it is to REVEAL that story. Revealing our story and some of the darker sides of who we are and what we have experienced was a formidable task and painful process. Our history is, well, our history. It's painful and muddled and often full of regrets. Why would I want to share that with anyone else?

For those of you brought up in a home where you didn't talk about things, and you just moved on, where even the thought of exposing yourself to be scrutinized by others was out of the question, maybe you're thinking, "I deal with things my own way" or "I've dealt with it already, and I've already forgiven that person" I challenge you to examine yourself. "Do you still feel the sting of past hurts? Are past offenses taking you out? Do you suffer from depression, guilt, anger, or anxiety?"

These are just a few of the symptoms revealed from unresolved issues that weigh us down as if we were carrying a bag of "ROCKS". For the purpose of the REVEAL process, I will refer to "ROCKS" as unresolved wounds and baggage we carry from our past into our present and future.

Part two of the R3 FACTOR is where we challenge individuals to "REWRITE" their story. Rewriting your story may require seeing the event from a different perspective. To REWRITE my story forces me to see what happened from another angle. I have to change my glasses. The glasses I saw through before the REVEAL process won't cut it anymore if I truly want to transform my life. We will explore REWRITE in depth in future chapters.

Part three of the R3 FACTOR is the journey of "RENEW." To RENEW is to make your life better than it ever was before. That pertains to making yourself, your relationships, and your spiritual walk better than it ever was, with the potential of being better than you could have imagined possible.

CHAPTER 2

LOVE, SEX AND MONEY

Love never dies a natural death. It dies because we don't know how to replenish its source. It dies of blindness and errors and betrayals. It dies of illness and wounds; it dies of weariness, of withering, of tarnishing. - Anais Nin

–Ron

Has it ever occurred to you this thing we call "relationship" requires a tremendous amount of work to figure out? Obstacles and roadblocks impede us at every turn—in fact, there are so many ways a relationship can go sideways, it's a wonder we even desire them.

Why can't relationships be easier? Why can't things sort themselves out just for once? Why do we run into the same old issues over and over and over without ever finding resolution? Albert Einstein suggested that insanity is doing the same thing over and over again and expecting different results—which is commonly done in relationships.

For the past twenty years plus, Tina and I have searched relentlessly to uncover the factors that make or break a relationship. We have observed, studied, and poured over research to determine why relationships are so challenging, hard and frustrating!

Is it possible there is an easier way to resolve conflict other than suffering on a therapist's sofa for ten years, evaluating just how messed up we really are?

We believe there are three dominant areas that affect and shape Relationships at the core level—Love, Sex, and Money. These three areas are not a comprehensive picture. We have discovered that when these areas are in alignment, along with a healthy and positive outlook, the road map of relationship is much easier to navigate. Divorces today are generally attributed to financial stress, a lack of physical attention or an inability to perceive what love really is. These three crucial areas will either make or break a relationship!

Let's Start with Love...

If we desire to be in relationship, maybe we need to backtrack a bit and figure out what love actually is. Maybe the reason love is so elusive and short lived is because none of us can agree upon what it is.

It's an old question—the meaning of love—from the first time man laid eyes on woman and the relationship between human beings commenced, people have been searching for the answer.

So, we decided to do a little research and headed over to the greatest library of all—GOOGLE! (How did we ever learn or find anything before Google?) "What is love" was the most searched phrase on Google in 2012, according to the company. The answers are surprising.

In an attempt to get to the bottom of the question once and for all, the *Guardian* gathered writers from the fields of science, psychotherapy, literature, religion and philosophy to give their definition of the much-pondered word.

The physicist, "Love is chemistry" Jim Al-Khalili

The psychotherapist, "Love has many guises" Philippa Perry

The philosopher, "Love is a passionate commitment"
Julian Baggini

The romantic novelist, "Love drives all great stories"
Jojo Moyes

The nun: "Love is free yet binds us" Catherine
Wybourne

Dictionary Definition of: love (lov) *n.¹*

1. A deep, tender, ineffable feeling of affection and solicitude toward a person, such as that arising from kinship, recognition of attractive qualities, or a sense of underlying oneness.

2. A feeling of intense desire and attraction toward a person with whom one is disposed to make a pair; the emotion of sex and romance.

Bible Definition: 1 Cor. 13 (NIV)

"Love is patient; love is kind; love is not envious or boastful or arrogant or rude. It does not insist on its own way; it is not irritable or resentful; it does not rejoice in wrongdoing, but rejoices in the truth. It bears all things, believes all things, hopes all things, endures all things. Love never ends."

I Corinthians 13, states that love is less of a feeling and more of an action. Love does. Love acts. Love chooses to go the extra mile.

As we pen this book, our desire is to clearly communicate our understanding of love to you in every language and by every definition. But the real test is when you **child proof it**—we dared to ask kids their definition of love. We believe their answers are as profound as some of the experts.

Children's answers to the question: **"What is Love?"**

–Nine-year old girl:

"Love is peace, joy and romance. It's a tingling feeling inside of you. You may like it or maybe not (if it's not a boy or girl that you like then you don't want to feel it)."

(We asked) How do you know you are loved?

"I know I'm loved by my family (be) cause they hug, kiss you and they look you in the eyes and tell you. You can tell because of the joy they bring to you. Peace is a relaxed feeling at home."

–Three-year-old girl

"Hearts and going to the park and reading books. When mommy holds me."

–Twelve-year-old boy

"When you like someone a lot, and they do stuff for you and WITH you. Love makes me feel happy and nice. Gifts REALLY make me feel loved."

The children's answers are simple yet poignant and maybe exactly what we are all looking for. Love looks a little different to each one of us and yet it is the same—acceptance, care, attention and affection. We have made this simple thing—of Love, far too complex.

Above all else, **Love is ultimately a choice.**

Let's talk about sex and or sexual frustration

–Ron and Tina

When speaking of intimacy, especially in our line of work as marriage experts, the auto response to what we are referring to is sex. To not disappoint you, sex is certainly a part of intimacy, but not the whole of it, because too many married couples engage in sex but never experience true intimacy.

Sex without intimacy quickly unravels a relationship. (And yes we know hook-ups and affairs can generate hot sex, but these are temporary and fleeting connections.) To have great sex in a committed relationship, you need intimacy.

So we hit the books again (okay, Google again).

"**Physical intimacy** is sensual proximity or touching. It is an act/reaction or an expression of feelings (such as genuinely strong/deep and close friendship, love, romantic infatuation/attraction or sexual attraction) which people have for one another. Examples of physical intimacy include being inside someone's personal space, holding hands, hugging, kissing, caressing, and sexual activity.

The forms of physical intimacy include physical closeness, touching (especially tenderly), touching intimate parts (including outer-course), and sexual penetration.

It is possible to be physically intimate with someone without actually touching them; however, certain proximity is necessary. For instance, a sustained eye contact is considered a form of physical intimacy, analogous to touching. When a person enters someone else's personal space for the purpose of being intimate, it is physical intimacy, regardless of the lack of actual physical contact.

Most people desire occasional physical intimacy, which is a natural part of human sexuality. Research has shown it has health benefits. A hug or touch can result in the release of oxytocin, dopamine, and serotonin, and a reduction in stress hormone levels." Wikipedia

We believe this is an awesome description of intimacy. We have personally experienced all of this at one time or another as a couple but also with friends when it comes to inviting them into our personal space. We know that intimacy, even when it comes to extended family and friends, requires a deeper knowing. In other words, the relationship must be safe.

Jesus developed a strong relationship with his disciples, yet it was not until the end of His ministry here on earth that He truly allowed them to come into an intimate relationship with Him. He told them He was going to share things with them that no one else was privy to. (John 15:15)

This is intimacy. It is a decision to allow another into your innermost space. Sexual intimacy takes it one step further by combining the physical with the emotional and spiritual. Finding true sexual freedom begins by discovering and rekindling intimacy.

As we move forward in the next few chapters into the REVEAL exercise, you may begin to see how an invitation to extended family members and friends into your personal space was not the healthiest decision you might have made or even the safest.

Having said this, if no one in your life qualifies as safe, then maybe you need to start asking yourself, "Why have I surrounded myself with unsafe people?"

As you continue to desire this intimacy, know that the REVEAL section is worth the reward as you discover the truth that sets you free. You deserve physical, emotional, and spiritual intimacy and getting honest is the first step.

Now about Money

"Show me the Money" might have propelled Jerry Maguire to fame and success, but in marriage—the tension of financial stress and constant bickering wears down the best relationships.

CHAPTER 3

REVEAL - "YOUR STORY"

When we are no longer able to change a situation - we are challenged to change ourselves. –Viktor E. Frankl

–Ron

The REVEAL stage is usually the most challenging portion of the three stages to get through for many people. If we are honest and if we allow God to show us what needs to be revealed, He will honor our desire through the gentleness of the Holy Spirit.

I'd like Tina to begin by sharing her journey of healing with you in hopes of helping you see the importance of the first step we all must take to truly heal. The first stage of the R3 FACTOR of great relationships is the REVEAL.

•*R1 - Reveal Yesterday*

–Tina

Home is where our story begins. In July of 2013, my husband was visiting close friends and preparing for a radio show with over 500,000 Internet listeners. While preparing for the show in their guest room, he glanced up and saw a picture on the wall of an idyllic home set in the woods with a white picket fence. There was an inscription above it: *"Home is where our story begins,"* the simple verse resonated deep within him. We build most of our seminars and speaking engagements within the paradigm of **"our story"** and the effect it has on each one of us. Our story determines our outlook and is our most powerful *life builder* or *life destroyer*. Each one of us has a unique and personal story and it began in our childhood home.

Our story is built on the foundation of our past—what we saw, heard and experienced as children. Our perceptions of love as we grew up and emotionally matured formed what we believe about love as adults. It is evident in the children's answers of what love is, that each love experience is unique and personal to the individual.

Although Ron and I are considered *relationship experts* and our work is in restoring relationships—we are distinctly different than most everyone in our industry because the main focus of our counseling, coaching and seminars is based on what the individual brings to the relationship table—the good, the bad and the ugly. We will lead you through an intensely personal journey of healing that will in turn transform your relational interactions.

Allow me to share part of my story, starting from the rockiest of beginnings—as I journeyed and, ultimately, discovered "what love is." I know my life was forever transformed the day I finally experienced the simplicity of love. From that day forward, I have seen thousands of lives experience the same freedom love brings, and I am thrilled to share this with you.

From early childhood until March of 1993, most of my life was permeated with toxic thoughts of feeling unloved and unaccepted. I couldn't answer the question, "What is love?" because every time I thought I had found love, it vanished as quickly as it appeared, leading to another painful heartbreak. Over and over, with each disappointment, my heart hardened to protect itself from the very thing it craved.

In our seminars, I refer to myself as a *master ROCK wall builder*. (I will share more on the *rocks* we pick up along life's journey in the next chapter) Over the years, as my family traveled throughout Europe, I was always in awe of the rock walls and fortresses I uncovered. Each wall was magnificently constructed with numerous shapes and differing sizes of rocks; and yet despite their awkward dimensions, these rocks were jammed perfectly together to form a wall that protected their territory. As I was looking at those walls, I stood in wonder how each rock was so different, yet the builder made them fit together to create a strong barrier. I remember staring at the wall and seeing myself behind it. I knew those walls well because I too was the master wall builder. I spent years carefully building my emotional walls. I had taken every wound, disappointment, multiple rejections, abandonment, feelings of being forgotten, anger, shame, guilt, and all those toxic emotions and built a rock wall of protection to guard myself from more offenders.

Every rock had a name or circumstance. The biggest rock that still plagues me today is the rock I named "CONTROL." Control had become my closest friend and ally. When life got chaotic and it seemed Control might be lost, *Anger*—my second best friend—would come to my aid to help me regain Control.

It was 1993 when my world and wall of rocks tumbled down. I felt like Humpty Dumpty sitting on my wall, feeling like the world couldn't hurt me or get to me, until the day the rock "Rejection" loosed itself from the well built wall and was thrown at my sweet, sweet baby girl, Jenny Michelle. Who am I? What kind of mother would throw a rock at her own daughter? What kind of mother could love one child more than the other? Still feeling like Humpty Dumpty who had a great fall; I felt like no one was going to be able to put me back together again.

I was enrolled in my first personal growth seminar along with my husband Ron. It was a five-day program guaranteed to *change your life* or you could get your money back. I desperately needed and craved for my life to change.

Upon arrival each person received a questionnaire, and as I began to answer the normal-run-of-the mill questions, my mind began to wander. I thought about what the weekend would hold for me: Could it be life changing? Would I really be free from the control that was taking a toll on my relationships? What about the anger and rejection, the loss, abandonment, and lack of forgiveness I lived with every day? What would become of all my rocks? Where would they go? Would I be able to love my daughter again?

An overwhelming burden of fear rested on my shoulders before I even entered the hotel ballroom that day. I realized I was going to be faced with the decision of saying goodbye to my two best friends—Control and Anger. These two were faithful friends that allowed me to bear hurtful events—Control would step in and create safety, and then Anger would protect me from the pain.

I continued filling out the questionnaire and a question struck me, "Tell us what your most painful memory as a child was?" As I wrote, the words tumbled out of me; the pen was imprinting words on the page, but the words did not seem like my own.

After what seemed like forever, I read what my hand had written, "My most painful memory as a child was when I was forgotten. How could they have forgotten me? They promised to come. Why? How could they leave me behind?"

I sat there, tears pouring down my face and realized we had yet to step through the ballroom door.

The moment I signed up for the seminar, I knew there was no going back. Ron, in all honesty, was simply tagging along to support me, but we both knew the real impetus for the weekend—was me!

So began an intense and emotionally provocative journey to self-discovery. Ron and I threw caution to the wind and fully immersed ourselves in the weekend despite our fears and despite our reluctance. I didn't have a clue what to expect and felt vulnerable and exposed just showing up. But I was committed. While the thought of change was terrifying, the thought of not changing was even more so.

Let me back up a couple of years so you can grasp why and how we chose to register for a five-day seminar in lieu of the exotic Hawaiian vacation we had saved and planned for over a year. Near the end of 1990, my eldest daughter Jenny (who was eight-years-old) began to show subtle signs of change. Although the alterations in her temperament were only evident to me, subconsciously I began to reject her. But it wasn't Jenny creating the distance between us, it was me. Jenny started to look like me and act like me. I could see as her body and personality developed all the things I hated about myself in her. She started gaining weight and this terrified me. I had avoided mirrors all my life and now it was like looking at my reflection when she was in front of me. With each day, the feeling grew more powerful and the wound sharper. To protect myself, I turned to *Anger* (my faithful friend) as a shield. And Anger was faithful—knowing I was prone to move towards Control in chaotic situations.

I couldn't bear another excruciating heartbreak—especially from my own child. This beautiful baby girl I had so desperately desired now appeared to be my enemy.

I treasured those first years of planting roots and building our little family. When Jenny was born, Ron worked for his brother Tom in the logging industry. We moved from Vancouver, British Columbia, back to the small town of Fruitvale, British Columbia, where Ron grew up when Jenny was a mere ten-days-old. I reveled in motherhood and homemaking. Jenny was like a delicate doll I couldn't bear to put down. I delighted in dressing her and playing house with baby by my side. Each moment with her was a precious gift. There were times I would wake her up before her nap was over, simply because I missed her.

Unlike my story, there wasn't a child more adored than my Jenny Michelle! For the first time in my life, I encountered unconditional love and it washed over me like a torrential downpour of emotion. Jenny was six-weeks-old when Ron's family generously hosted a baby shower in our new home. My baby girl was passed from one set of arms to the next as everyone *oohed* and *aahhed* over her peaceful countenance. Finally, the time came when she was returned back into mama's arms. I felt her tiny body relax into my chest as she opened her eyes, looked deeply into mine, sighed in utter contentment, and then nestled herself back against me and fell asleep.

My heart exploded. The moment imprinted on my soul, and for the first time I felt truly wanted, chosen and loved above everyone else. This precious baby chose me.

So what happened to mar this beautiful story? Well dear reader...this is what I asked myself for almost two years. I secretly grieved as I tried to conceal the feelings of rejection I felt towards her. I couldn't do the normal "mommy" things naturally. There was no ease in hugging and laughing and holding her—but dis-ease, and I feared people would see through my facade and find out I was a sham. Every day I would go about meeting her physical needs but emotionally I was drowning in a world of guilt and shame for what I was doing to our precious baby girl. Now *Guilt* and *Shame* had attached to my spirit to join the other host of coping mechanisms I dragged around like a backpack. Add in *Justification*, another friend who helped me not feel so horrible about myself, when I saw the longing in her eyes for her mommy.

Sometimes, even now, I am haunted by the sadness I saw in Jenny's eyes, but I remind myself those emotions only steal from the present. Toxic emotions rob us of our health, destroy us personally, and cause havoc in our relationships. Dr Caroline Leaf, a neuroscientist and author of the book, "Who Switched off My Brain?" suggests our heart was not created to carry an abundance of negative emotions instead she says in her book, *we were wired for love.* It is this kind of toxicity that will literally kill us – *"87% to 95% of the illnesses that plague us today are a direct result of our thought life. What we think about affects us physically and emotionally."*

The secret was out about one year in. My daughter went to spend the weekend at my sister's house, which was always a treat as her cousins were all fairly close in age. My sister seemed to have a real authentic and close relationship with her three children. She was the kind of mom I wanted to be—open and safe. She and her children could easily talk about anything.

It was in the midst of one of these *talks*—with all girls piled on the bed, when Jenny knew the feelings of rejection, separation, and disconnection she had were real. After an evening talking, connecting, and sharing her heart with her cousins Sarah, Rachel, and her Auntie Brigitte, Jenny discovered something was missing in our home. When they headed to bed she asked her cousins, "Does your mom always talk to you like that?"

"Yes, of course!" they replied. Jenny was amazed, and in her pain she proceeded to later ask her auntie, "Why does my mommy love my brother Josh more than me?"

So, we come to the big question once again, *"What is love?"* It seems, in this instance, for Jenny, love was a deep connection with her mom. Jenny also recognized that her brother experienced it while she did not.

My sister wasted no time in confronting me on what I was desperately trying to hide from the world. It didn't help that my husband was an elder in our church, and I was the children's pastor. We had certain images to maintain, and weakness wasn't something I wanted to advertise. While I instructed children each Sunday on God's love, and reminded them to honor their mother and father, I was hiding the painful truth of what was going on in my own home.

This might be your story too—with different details and different anguish—but the secret pain and internal struggle resonate within you. You think you can conceal the truth and tightly stuff your pain under a smile, but while the world might buy it for a time, it won't take long before our hidden secrets will be brought to light.

I finally took my sister's counsel and sought help. But it was help I was not ready for.

I was directed to one of the best counselors in our city for therapy. I was petrified yet excited. I deeply desired to love and nurture my little girl again. I yearned to show her what love was and connect with her. So, off I went to my first appointment where the counselor listened as I shared my story with him. He offered me hope and a light at the end of my very dark tunnel.

I went home energized and relieved. The counselor sent me home with an assignment—specifically geared towards my emotions and pulling out the root causes of pain from my childhood. While I know now he was trying to lead me towards healing, he didn't know the can of worms he was opening with his request.

The second session one week later was not so amicable for me. We discussed the homework and this part went well, but about mid-way through our hour he turned the conversation towards my mother issues. I quite calmly reminded him why I was there, and it was not to go back thirty years. I also told him, in no uncertain terms, that I already dealt with my past (remember, I was the master wall builder) and spent many years putting it behind me where it belonged.

I think I even quoted a Bible verse where the Apostle Paul said in Philippians 3:13, we are instructed to "Forget what is behind and strain toward what is ahead." Clearly, this didn't go well for me. The counselor looked at me and said, "Well, I'm not sure how that is working for you, because you seem to be taking what happened to you as an innocent child and now as an adult are putting it on your child."

Had he ended there I would have smiled and nodded and secretly proceeded to pile another rock in my wall that had now become a fortress. But, he went on to say that a *child's core need is acceptance and rejection is the deepest wound for a child to overcome.*

He said we can heal from physical, verbal and even sexual abuse much easier than we can from rejection—especially from a parent.

His words annihilated me. Now I had not only *Guilt* and *Shame* on my shoulders but outer *Devastation* as well. As much as the counselor offered me hope, FEAR had me bound and tied in thick knots. There was no way I was capable of moving the rocks in my wall that took over thirty years to build. I went for one more session, hoping he would give up on the thought of going back and would simply help me move forward. What I didn't know then, but Ron and I teach now, is that unresolved issues in your past will always rear their ugly heads. No matter how many rock walls you have built, these toxic thoughts and emotions will come back to haunt you in the most inopportune way and wreak havoc in your relationships. The rock walls can't keep out new pain, hurts, or even the past. They just keep us from intimacy and relational success in the present.

As you are taking in and internalizing this chapter my dear reader, I wish I was there with you to encourage you! Do not let fear bind you as it did me over twenty years ago. Make the decision to engage in the REVEAL process; full disclosure is not a choice but a mandate when it comes to healing. You cannot change or heal what you do not reveal and bring into the light.

One more year went by and now Jenny was ten-years-old. The rejection continued to get worse and life at the Konkins' was not fun with all the toxic activity swirling around us.

God bless my dear sister as she never gave up on me, and I pray you have a special someone in your life who will not give up on you. Maybe this book is your special *someone* and you did not pick it up by accident. This book is saying in very clear terms, "DON'T GIVE UP," even when you believe you have tried everything.

My sister knew the counseling had not been well received, so she encouraged me to try a different tactic. She had heard of a five-day intensive program, owned by Dr. Phil McGraw, that was coming to our city of Vancouver, BC.

So with a sliver of hope and great trepidation we embarked on the journey of healing—and healing it was.

CHAPTER 4

REVEAL - REJECTION

Rejection leaves you with a broken heart. You drive yourself crazy with every question you can think of —what, why, how come—and then your sadness turns to anger. —Tina Konkin

—Tina

Again, as much as I would love to move on, it would be unfair to you as a reader if I didn't explain why LOVE didn't have permanent residency in my heart. Although I deeply desired to love and be loved, I couldn't make it stick. Love had nowhere to land—no resting place to root. It was as if my heart's foundation was built on sand. And so, with each storm that arose, or sometimes merely a gentle wind, my capacity to accept and give love would be shaken to the core, leaving a pile of rubble and heartache along with more devastation.

I approached life and made choices through the lens and aches of my childhood. I can't stress enough how our past affects us—the things we see, hear, and experience, both positive and negative from our childhood will be the foundation we build on as an adult. If our wounds or false beliefs are left unresolved, these wounds will re-open under duress and negatively shape how we love.

It didn't occur to me that my current situation might be a reflection of my past, nor did I want to entertain the thought.

It was only a matter of time before I turned to food to cope with the shame. Any time painful thoughts of my daughter and the growing distance between us intruded, I turned to food for comfort. It was an old coping mechanism I turned to in times of despair. Eating comforted me as a child when I couldn't bear the pain of rejection or loss and abandonment.

I was eight-years-old when I discovered food and how it could so easily numb the pain. Was it a coincidence that Jenny was eight-years-old too when this rejection cycle started? Though my rejection started before I was born, I was eight years old when my parents moved our family from Belguim to Canada, and it was the following two years that were the most painful for me as a child. I have asked myself these questions on numerous occasions, and although I'm not 100% certain, the correlation is too close to not consider. After a year of trying to brush my issues under the rug, I woke up one morning and faced my distressing reality. I walked into the bathroom, splashed water on my face, and glanced at my reflection in the mirror. I had gained eighty pounds in the course of a year, and my face appeared tired and weary from the emotional burden I carried. I looked into the eyes staring back at me and promised myself I was done running. I was tired of hurting myself, my family, my husband and most of all my children.

Following through on my promise, Ron and I promptly registered for the five-day personal growth seminar2 I spoke of in Chapter 3. The conference marked a pivotal change in the direction of my life. I forced my overwhelming FEAR to take a back seat; I finally confronted the past, my demons, and all the feelings of rejection I stuffed deep inside. This time, I didn't run away or ignore the issues at the root of my troubles. I stood my ground and with determination, took the necessary steps to truly understand everything buried inside of me. For the first time in my life, I began to breathe easier and operate in freedom.

When the feeling of fear left me, I was finally able to forgive my parents, the kids at school who mocked me, and even the people who had died and abandoned me. (Isn't it crazy how rejection blames even the dead?) Most of all, I was able to forgive myself for the damage I caused my precious baby girl.

I came to understand why I rejected my own daughter. I realized that in my brokenness I saw myself in her—the little eight-year-old girl who was forgotten. As Jenny started looking more and more like me and began to put on a little weight, I began to see her future through my old pain and it was not acceptable to me. This lack of control over my own past brought up anger. I had worked too hard over the years to bury this pain only to be faced by it again in the face of an eight-year-old child.

And therein lies the problem—I had buried the pain not resolved it. Whatever we do not resolve from the past will find a way to resurface in the most in-opportune times; hence, we hurt our self and our relationships. Love does not bury the truth, but instead reveals it, so that we can REWRITE our story. Rewriting our story takes what is revealed and gives it a new slant and a new purpose.

Today, my daughter is over thirty years of age and we share a love that is deeper than our challenges, our misunderstandings, and my mistakes as a mom. It is a love that is pure and cannot be shaken. It is a love that is real and built on a solid foundation.

I will give you a better picture of how rejection affected my own life in a later chapter. But for now, dear reader, if you are still reading this book, dare to confront your past so love can flow in and out of you. Both you and your family deserve to be loved and accepted.

CHAPTER 5

REVEAL - THE
GIANT ERASER

*"The past is a great place and I don't want to
erase it or to regret it, but I don't want to be its
prisoner either." Mick Jagger*

I WOULDN'T CHANGE ONE DAY

–Tina

As I sit here and ponder what to share to best inspire
you to embark on your own personal journey of
healing. I find my desire is to bring hope to you who as

children experienced the pain of a broken heart. For many, like me, there may have been a reality of growing up under the umbrella of rejection, thereby feeling unwanted and like a burden. Maybe you too felt like you should never have been born. Or maybe like Ron, you felt like you always missed the mark and were never good enough, even though you grew up in a happy and loving family.

At forty-two-years old (after seven years of growth had already passed), God and I had a moment, where I recognized I wouldn't change a day of my life, painful or otherwise. It took forty-two years to get to this place of acknowledgment that my pain had a purpose. I finally understood that I would not change a thing on the storyboard of my life. That moment made me realize I could turn my pain—my journey, my story, and my life— into a gift of healing and hope to others. By transforming my pain into a gift, I could offer this ability to choose healing to many hurting adults with similar child-like emotions.

How can I even describe this emotion? It was an amazing feeling when I fully grasped that all things can and will be worked out for good. As a Christian, I understood theologically this concept and in theory believed it, but it became real the day God and I were looking at my storyboard and He opened my eyes to His perspective.

–Ron

Let's take a moment and explain the concept of a storyboard and its significance.

A storyboard is a graph of life events—both painful and joyful. *See diagram at the end of this chapter.* Every high and every low, starting from your birth is plotted on the board.

It's an eye-opening exercise, because what we saw, heard and experienced in our past will often take root in our heart. When you take a moment, truly be still, and allow yourself to reflect on your life, the moments that caused the deepest pain and hurt are revealed to you even though you may have brushed them aside.

This action of brushing aside painful memories, or ignoring them, can be so severe that it is difficult to acknowledge these have any present effect on your emotions and behaviors.

But remember, Tina and I believe in the relational law of, "What goes in will come out". All of what you saw, heard and experienced developed your belief system. It also counts for who you are today and how you operate in your relationships. I remember Tina telling me about a good friend of her family, whom they called Uncle Jack. He was from Australia and apparently sounded just like Crocodile Dundee. He would say to the kids, "Garbage in, garbage out, so be careful what you let in." So, in memory of Uncle Jack, think about all the toxic garbage you let in, it will often find a release valve in behaviors that are harmful both to ourselves and those we are in relationship with.

–Tina

In the storyboard exercise, I began to see glimpses of pain I had brushed aside and did not think were relevant (due to more obvious sources of pain from physical and sexual abuse). While examining my storyboard, I became angry, but strangely enough it was not anger at the people who hurt or abused me, instead the anger was directed at God.

This was a different emotion! I had always thought of God as my safety net, but here I was looking at the storyboard with red hot anger bubbling up inside me. With a sudden jerk of my head, my eyes traveled from the words I wrote on the paper up to the ceiling. I pointed my finger at God, and asked, "Why? How could you? Where were you?"

The tears fell hot on my face and my familiar friend Anger simmered in my heart, but this time the finger was pointed at God. As I opened my eyes and looked up, I saw a vision of God's hand appearing through the ceiling. In his hand was a giant eraser.

In that moment, it felt like God was handing me a giant eraser and giving me permission, like a teacher to a student, to erase whatever events I wanted to. With this permission, I felt He was promising that I would feel like it had never happened. Imagine how this felt. Imagine being given permission to erase the pain and hurt. For years I had been carrying huge rocks, some the size of boulders, so heavy the pain tore at and crushed my shoulders. Each day these rocks called Anger, Rejection, Resentment and Un-forgiveness weighed me down and blocked true intimacy from my life.

Now, imagine being given permission to throw off all that weight that caused these toxic emotions. I could erase it all!

In that moment, my mind flashed to a different life—one of living in joy, peace, acceptance, and forgiveness. All those ugly and painful memories could be erased for good. I braced myself and with great excitement, grabbed the eraser, and searched for the first memory to banish. This gift of erasing was tremendous! I could hardly contain my excitement.

The first memory I confronted was of my mom crying because she was pregnant. Of course I would erase this day, so I would never again replay those words, "You should never have been born."

Something stopped me, as my eyes jumped to a time where, as a little girl I went into the boy's bathroom and was laughed at by my classmates. Then I remembered THE DAY MY FRIENDS FORGOT ME, and again, my mind skipped to the day I found out my husband had an affair. This one was going to take a huge eraser, and as I raised my hand to erase all these painful memories, something strange happened. I lifted the eraser and handed it back to God, surrendering those events and the experiences back to Him. As I surrendered it all to God, a calm settled upon my heart. I couldn't believe what was happening, that feeling of peace was indescribable. I closed my eyes to enjoy the moment, it was then I realized all of these events made up my story.

These pieces of my life, whether they were good or bad, painful or full of joy, made me who I am. I sat back and asked myself, "Would I be the woman I am today if I used the eraser?" As in any classic time travel movie, if you go back in time and change an event, there is a direct correlation to the future, and any change can alter the future drastically. I accepted, like the picture-perfect painting hanging on the wall in our friends' guest room, "Home is Where Our Story Begins." It was in this moment when my heart truly understood what true surrender to a good God was. It was then I made the decision that Living Above the Line was a decision I could make in spite of my painful past.

The line I speak of, and a phrase we use in our coaching practice, is this idea of *Living Above the Line.* The line is what sets apart choosing to operate in positive or negative emotions. The Line is our REALITY. If we do not acknowledge our present reality we cannot change or heal from our past. Every day is a choice to live in REALITY or denial.

I had wasted enough years Living Below the Line in anger, rejection, resentment, guilt, shame, blame, bitterness and FEAR! By accepting my reality that my heart was filled with toxic emotions, I was able to begin my journey of healing. In the words of my husband, I "get to" live the life I have been given because I wake up each morning with another breath.

For that I am blessed and will choose to *Live Above the Line*. *Living Above the Line* where there is joy, love, peace, intimacy, forgiveness, acceptance, purity, truth, dreams, purpose and COMPASSION.

> *"One cannot and must not try to erase the past merely because it does not fit the present."*
> *Golda Meir*

As I stated earlier, during this process, I came to peace with my past and no longer desired to change my life. As I looked over the storyboard, I could see the experiences of my life written out and traces of emotions stirred from those memories. Yet, seeing everything from a big picture view helped me from getting sucked into a whirlpool of emotions surrounding one painful memory, which is often what happens when encountering one memory at a time. I came to understand that, despite the intensity of certain painful experiences, everything happened for a reason, and I had been protected and guided through the storms. Looking through each memory, I began to understand that every nick, cut, and bruise on my heart and spirit was a powerful reminder of something I had overcome. And the scars made me stronger and more compassionate towards others.

I recognized I was trying to run this race of life while stopping to pick up every rock or pebble I encountered along the way. None of those rocks helped me run any faster or with more energy; needless to say, they did quite the opposite. However, that day I knew a huge burden had been lifted. When I surrendered all the pain, I felt as if I could run around the world and never grow tired.

Slowly, but surely, I began to give thanks for the struggles that helped me grow in strength and wisdom and helped me find purpose. Through this epiphany, I discovered I could turn defeat into triumph, loss into victory, and pain into empowerment. I realized I wanted to share this magnificent gift of healing and hope with others. There are so many who have suffered the pain of emotional trauma during childhood and many others that, despite their great circumstances, never felt good enough.

How many times had I read the scripture stating that all things can and will be worked out for good? How many times had I read it and, in the thralls of despair, tossed this ribbon of hope out the window? However, in the moment of that revelation, I not only understood the incredible power of this promise, but I felt it. It permeated my entire being. I felt renewed.

I was now ready to take each rock of my past, one at a time, and remove them from the Great Wall of Tina. Through gratitude and forgiveness and trust in God's goodness, I could now find purpose in my pain. I could now experience true intimacy. I could now give and receive love freely and deeply.

Tina's Storyboard

- *Jesus is always my friend*
- *Getting married*
- *Jesus loves me*
- *Having kids*
- *99% on test*
- *Going home to Belgium*
- *The pool with mom*
- *College*
- *Italy, Gandma's house*
- *Choices seminar*
- *Ice cream in a carton*
- *Clubbing, being popular*
- *Cancer*

- *Jesus is here, too!*
- *Cancer*
- *1st Vow*
- *Leaving Belgium*
- *99% on test*
- Mom's disapproval
- *Jim's Death*
- *Boys bathroom*
- *Going home to Belgium*
- *2nd Vow*
- *Mom's pregnant*
- *3rd Vow*
- *Forgotten*
- *Ron's Affair*
- *Fire Poker*
- *Sexual abuse over and over*
- *Getting FAT*

CHAPTER 6

REVEAL - DISAPPOINTMENT & ANGER

Your "Where there is anger, there is always pain underneath."–Eckhart Tolle

–Tina

I looked over my storyboard, certain events stood out as incredibly painful. I knew I needed to explore these stories further and dig deeper to discover the source of pain I associated with them.

Here is an example of a story (first identified in my storyboard) I wrote about being forgotten. The toxic feelings I associated with it needed to be revealed so I could find true healing.

Disappointment ~ Ten-years-old

The Living Room Window

My father had been working very hard at his job and he had also been working to establish a relationship with his boss so he could get a promotion. One week, his boss invited all of us for a family dinner at his house. My father was really excited about this opportunity to "get in good" with his boss. I was just as excited as my father was that night because I had heard my father's boss had children my age. On the way to our destination, I sat in the car and anxiously wondered if I would get along with the other kids. I had been so lonely at school and yearned to have new friends.

As soon as my family entered into the atrium of the house, I saw the children I had heard about—two girls. I stood by the door and waited bashfully until our parents introduced us. As soon as the introductions were over, the girls looked up at their mother and asked if we could go play. After she gave a quick assent, I looked up at my own mother and got a quick nod. The girls waved their hands for me to follow, and they led me to their playroom. A smile was glued to my face the entire time, and I was brimming over with joy. It had been so long since I had anybody to play with and I liked feeling included. The girls laughed at my jokes and didn't make fun of me if I did something silly.

I heard the sound of vaguely familiar laughter in my ears. It struck me that I was hearing my own laughter. I hadn't heard it in such a long time. Sure, there were times I laughed at a joke here and there, but not so prolonged and loud as I heard myself laughing at that moment. What made me happier than having somebody to play with was that the girls really liked me.

We heard it was time for us to go home, and then one of the girls ran up to her mother and asked her, "Can Tina come with us to the movies tomorrow? Please, please, please!" She held her clasped hands under her chin and bounced up and down on her toes.

My heart sank as soon as I heard the question. My parents raised my sister and me with a strict religious upbringing and we weren't allowed to do many of the things our peers were able to do, like going to the movies. Every Saturday, all the kids from school would go to movie matinees together, but my sister and I were never allowed to go.

The girls' mother smiled sweetly and said, "Yes, of course! Is it alright if Tina goes with us to the movies tomorrow? There's a 1 o'clock movie showing so I can drop by at noon to pick her up." All eyes turned to my parents. It may have seemed like a simple question to the girls and their mother, but for me, it was pivotal. I held my breath and watched my parents exchange a look between them. My mother turned back to their mother with a grin and said, to my surprise, "Yes, so we'll see you at noon." They were willing to set aside their strict rules to establish a good relationship with my father's boss.

I could barely sleep that night. Not only did I have new friends that I was going to see again tomorrow, but I was going to see my first movie at the theater! "What am I going to wear tomorrow?" I wondered. "Is this going to become a weekly event?" "Will I finally get to be like the other kids at school?" "Maybe if I can go to the movies, I'll have more friends." A constant stream of thoughts ran through my mind until my eyelids grew heavy and I finally fell asleep.

Morning finally arrived. I quietly got out of bed so as to not wake my sister and shuffled to the closet to pick out my outfit. I washed up hastily and was ready to go by about 8 o'clock in the morning. I made my way to the living room window that looked out over the driveway. I fixed my eyes on the street and prepared myself to wait.

My mother walked into the living room and a quizzical expression crossed her face when she saw me sitting at the window. "I don't want to miss them," I explained in my defense. She didn't respond and walked past me into the kitchen. I could hear her cooking in the background, but my focus remained intent on the driveway. I began to picture their car pulling up and my two new friends hopping out of the car, overwhelmed with excitement to see me.

As the clock ticked closer to noon, I began to squirm in my seat. My legs had gone numb from sitting for so long, but I remained fixed to my spot. My heart started to flutter with expectation at noon, but still no car pulled up to the driveway. The hour dragged slowly by until 1 o'clock came without any sign of the girls and their mother. The movie had already started. "Maybe they're running late," I reassured myself. When the clock struck 2 o'clock, I realized there was no hope. They had forgotten me. I hid my face and ran to my room. I buried my face in my pillow and sobbed. I couldn't understand why or how they could forget me; I thought they had liked me. Not only did I feel insignificant, but I felt foolish for thinking they wanted me to be their friend.

Fast-forward to 1993, as I sat outside the ballroom tears pouring down my face.

So you see, dear reader, it's not always the most significant events from an adult perspective that affect us so painfully; but to a ten-year-old, that day imprinted a strong emotional message not to be forgotten on my heart. Even though I rarely thought of the painful event, its negative effect poured over into all the relationships that followed over the years. I carried a sense of insignificance, and I believed I didn't matter enough to be remembered for a simple matinée.

In the dynamics of my relationship with Ron, the fear of being forgotten is still prevalent. Even in a grocery store, if he wandered off it would trigger an anger neither of us understood. Ron would not react well and, to be honest, he really wondered if I was a few fries short of a Happy Meal. "Really?" he would say, "You honestly think I would just leave you here?"

Then he would add, "Even if I did forget you, you have a cell phone; you can call me, or worst case scenario, you could call a cab." I would get angrier as he used his logic. He'd always add in the final jabs of humiliation, "You're a big girl." But, really, psychologically speaking, in that moment, when the familiar feeling came back of being forgotten, I was not a big girl.

Let me explain so you can understand how this theory has the power to heal if you will grasp it. When a trauma— physical, emotional or spiritual—takes place, no matter how significant or insignificant the event may seem, your mind interprets the pain not on how big or small the wounding event was but how it affected you. So as an adult, when an event triggers that same feeling, you go back to the age of the original event and you react with the same emotion the child had. This is why we put such importance on the REVEAL stage. If you are at all like me, you have events in your past that are dictating some of your unhealthy mental, emotional, and spiritual reactions based on the wounding of your past.

Anger - The Fire Poker

–Tina

Part of my REVEAL was identifying when my friend Anger first appeared in my life to help me through situations I could not control. So here are the facts I have uncovered—and pieced together from stories told over the years.

My parents met at a young age, my mom was only fourteen and my dad was eight years older. They were married within two years and started their marriage with incredible financial debt. They resided in Belgium when my mother got pregnant with me. Since my parents needed to earn a double income in order to catch up with all of their financial commitments, my father's parents moved from Italy to help look after me. My grandparents cared for me under the roof of their son and daughter-in-law despite the fact they felt like intruders. Nine months later, my grandparents—Nonno and Nonna, as I came to call them—decided to return to Italy and I went with them. Life was comfortable in Italy and they poured all of their love and devotion into me.

When I was eighteen-months-old, my father boarded a train from Belgium and traveled to Italy as the distance between us had grown too great. He spent a week with his parents and attempted to rekindle his bond with me. We went on long walks; he spoiled me with candy and ice cream as we traversed about the town. He decided it was time to start the journey home as he was due back at work. The journey included me going home with him.

The day soon arrived for us to return to Belgium. Nonna dutifully packed the bags full of toddler necessities, but she could not bear to come to the train station to say goodbye. But Nonno actually boarded the train and went as far as Rome with us (about a three-hour train ride). The first leg of the train ride with Nonno on board passed without consequence. However, if Nonno disembarking wasn't enough, the situation quickly deteriorated when I became hungry and my father realized the milk had become rotten. He was overwhelmed, and I was inconsolable. I imagine I finally fell asleep from pure exhaustion and I'm pretty sure it was quite the relief for a young dad traveling alone.

Once we reached Belgium, my dad took me to an unfamiliar place that he called "home." The anxiety mounted in me as more time passed and the realization began to sink in that I wouldn't be seeing my grandparents for a long time. My dad then introduced me to a woman I didn't recognize. He called her my "mother." In my little toddler mind, I couldn't register this woman as a maternal figure. My Nonna was mother to me. She had held me in her arms anytime I needed comfort, and it was she who I yearned for in that moment. Since my father had to return to work, he left me with "mother," and I was now alone with a complete stranger. My mother looked at me, unsure of what to do. Her uncertainty fed my own fear, and I moved away from her to keep my distance. I didn't feel safe and it wasn't fair.

My poor seventeen-year-old mom tired of us just standing there staring at each other, tried to interact with me, insisting we play a game. But when she tried to approach me, my anxiety flared into anger. I ran blindly away from her into the dining room. It was beautifully decorated with a brand new dining set. I ran behind it and grabbed a poker from beside the fireplace and began swinging it around me. It wasn't long before it made contact with one of her new dining chairs. The impact was satisfying to me and I struck it again. Each blow etched my fury into the wood. My body was hot with rage and my mind was reeling in confusion. "Who is this woman?" "Where are Nonno and Nonna?" "Why am I here?"

Though I was only eighteen-months-old, I can still see the expression of shock on my mother's face. Her mouth and eyes were frozen wide open as she watched this tiny little girl unleash so much anger. She stood there helpless with her arms hanging limply by her side as I landed blow after blow on the chairs. I didn't stop until my body was exhausted from the exertion, finally collapsing on the floor. Yet, my grip remained firm on the poker.

Just as I held tightly on to the instrument of anger that day, I continued to live my life holding on to Anger as a shield. It became my initial line of defense when confronted with pain or confusion. It allowed me to shut out the rest of the world and relegate me to a bubble where I could be protected—or so I thought. I was always on guard and ready to lash out if I had the slightest inclination someone was intent on hurting me. Though Anger was rooted in me for many years, I now know it was not my friend, and it did far more harm than good. More often than not, my anger pushed away the people I loved the most. Although I have come a long way, I still catch myself reverting to anger when I am ignored, pushed, or cornered. But now I am quick to push away the toxic thoughts, knowing Anger and Resentment will only cause more damage to me than any perceived enemy.

I hope you will make the decision to face each ROCK that has formed your walls and cut you off from enjoying today and loving those around you. It is time for you to break down your walls.

CHAPTER 7

REVEAL - "EDDIE'S BOX"

"He was the last of five to come
He was the center like the sun
His life cut short like the morning dew
A brother that I never knew"
—Ron Konkin

–Ron

I have always had it in my heart to help people and to see them set free from pain, even as a young boy growing up. From my earliest memories, our home was filled with people –hurting people, especially kids. You see, my mom and dad were foster parents, and they had a burden for hurting people as well.

When I was around five or six years old, I was exploring in our three bedroom farm house in southern British Columbia. I was in my dad and mom's closet looking for treasures. Instead of coming across a treasure, hidden away deep in the back of the closet was a little box. I opened it and there in the box I found pictures. I couldn't see very well in the closet, so I stepped out into the light and perched myself on the bed.

This is how I became acquainted with the youngest of my older brothers. His name was Eddie. Prior to my discovery I had only seen one picture of him in the house. It was his first birthday he was sitting on the grass with a huge cake in front of him. I saw a picture of me as well, and Eddie and I looked identical, as if we were twins. The only person who could tell us apart was mom. As I began to gaze at the pictures in the little box, sadness washed over me.

My discovery that day was what we affectionately call "Eddie's box". There in the box were pictures of little Eddie in his casket surrounded by my mom and dad and my siblings.

In my journey of REVEAL many years later, remembering those pictures had a profound effect on me. Not necessarily in a negative way, but it did give me an understanding of the sadness I had seen in my mom's eyes as a young boy. It also gave me an understanding of my father's anger –often directed at me.

Even though there was pain in our household, mom and dad overcame much of it—through their faith and trust in God. Their mission was—to take broken kids from broken homes and show them the love of Christ. Was it always done right? No, not even close. Was it a perfect home? Absolutely not! But we did learn how to give, how to be a family, and most importantly, how to love and serve The Lord.

In all of our brokenness, there was also hurt. I came out of my home angry and with a resentful heart towards my father. My father passed many good gifts to his children but I would be remiss in not acknowledging the negative trait of anger I received from him. I in turn brought anger into my relationship with Tina and seemed destined to pass it on to my children.

The REVEAL is such an important step towards healing, and I was deathly afraid of it. I was only eighteen-years-old when I met Tina and twenty-years-old when we married.

I always say she *robbed the cradle* since she is a couple of years older than me. I was naive and inexperienced and I was not ready for the onslaught of a very strong and confident woman, whom her college mates accurately described: "Tina goes where angels fear to tread".

I, on the other hand was not like that, which is exactly why I was attracted to her. I knew if we were ever in trouble, Tina would be able to handle it. Tina was smart. She had traveled the world already, was a child evangelist and a speaker. I was merely a dumb logger who fell off the tractor and had somehow landed this incredible woman.

Looking back at those early years, I was like a deer in the headlights; not really sure of what was coming next. And what would come next was not what any young married couple would expect. There were countless fights, power struggles, disappointments, unmet expectations, and an insecurity on my part of how to make her happy.

I had married into a family where money and business were of the utmost importance. I liked the alluring attraction it created even though I never felt I measured up.

Unfortunately, the very things I once loved and was in awe of about my wife –her take-action and controlling approach, soon became a huge obstacle in our relationship. I began to resent Tina because I felt I had no control, no say. All the decisions were made for me, either by her or her family. These feelings were not new to me. I had experienced similar feelings in the years prior growing up with a father who yelled and at times belittled me –for getting the wrong wrench, or stalling the tractor, or just about burning down the barn (well maybe I deserved that one). It was the same feeling, just a different time and space.

When Tina would tell me do something, it was like my dad said it. Or when she confronted me on an issue I had no answer for or did not want to fess up to, again, it was like my dad cornering me. Many times it would be something as simple as commenting how I loaded the dishwasher. I would rise up in anger and lash out at her. It was the only defense I knew. I had no other tools to use. I was in constant defense mode.

Years of turf wars continued between Tina and I. It wasn't all bad, but the very foundation of our relationship eroded away. We did agree on a few major points. One of them was our faith, (I'll come back to that in a later chapter) and the "D" word was never to be used in our home, however, killing each other was not out of the question.

As the years passed by –Jenny and Josh arrived, we matured in our relationship, and we attended an amazing five-day course (Tina has already mentioned) which absolutely changed my life. We established ourselves in the personal growth and development industry and then at year seventeen, I just about threw everything in the toilet.

Even though we had done a great deal of work on ourselves, I had not taken care of my core issues. I still had never truly forgiven my dad. The resentment which had built up towards Tina in the earlier years had never been dealt with. I had not forgiven her, even though I "loved" her more than ever before. I had everything going for me –our business was a huge success and our family was intact, yet I allowed another woman into my heart compromising all that was truly important.

That year, I cheated on Tina. We will look at this in more detail in later chapters as to why something like this can occur in seemingly good relationships.

Like I said earlier, the REVEAL stage is not easy. For some of us, it can be complex and intricate. It's like going in for surgery, the doctor opens you up and steps back because it's more complicated than he first anticipated.

There are areas of our past we may believe have nothing to do with the present but we know from both personal experience and as relationship coaches, this couldn't be further from the truth.

The past has everything to do with our present.

Are you willing to look at some of your damage from the past, and begin to connect the dots as to how those experiences still have a profound effect on you today?

You see, revealing is merely the beginning of an amazing journey of discovery that will have a profound effect on your life.

There is freedom in truth.

Oh, it may hurt for a time because your emotional being or your soul man has been stuck in the past for so long. You see, most people (unknowingly) continue to live in their past. They continue to live in the rejection, anger, bitterness, abuse, denial, self-loathing, insecurity, and so many more negative feelings.

When we have these toxic feelings and negative reactions we tend to lash out at those we are in relationship with. That is not only unfair it is wrong.

You can continue to blame others for where you are today. You can smolder in the dimming coals of your once bright life and future, or you can "man up" or "woman up" and take accountability for what you are feeling today.

Being truly happy and content means, "I take accountability for my own feelings and where they originate. I do what is necessary and encourage my soul to mature."

Most of us are stuck with these immature child-like emotions in an adult body. This is a recipe for disaster! Connecting the dots means I recognize that these feelings are not because my husband or wife is a complete and utter jerk. Take into consideration this question when you are not in a toxic emotional state: Do you believe your partner's intention is to make your life miserable? Could it be that they either have no clue or don't know why you are reacting like a psychotic person? Perhaps you have not revealed to yourself or your partner what is happening on the inside of you when they do certain things to trigger your damage.

Revealing is an ongoing process in all of us. We will always have things to explore in our intricate and complicated lives, but we can't just stay in the REVEAL stage. This would be too depressing and painful.

CHAPTER 8

REVEAL - INTIMACY

Passion is the quickest to develop, and the quickest to fade. Intimacy develops more slowly, and commitment more gradually still. –Robert Sternberg

–Tina

In marriage, one of the biggest areas of tension can be in the bedroom. The REVEAL stage is crucial when it comes to building intimacy and yes –a better sex life!

I want to share with you how the REVEAL looked in my life in the area of intimacy. When I lived under the umbrella of rejection, intimacy was a struggle for me. While the physical act of sex was pleasurable, the touchy-feely part of intimacy was not. Ron could only get so far into my heart and then I would lock up. It was like an instant wall of rocks that went up. I never fully let him into my personal space. As a matter of fact I didn't let anyone into my space, not him, not the children, nor my family or friends. The risk of being hurt, rejected, or abandoned was too painful.

And then along came Ron's infidelity at year seventeen, the same year I proclaimed, I can't believe you are my man and God has chosen me to be your wife. Ron you have surpassed any dream of what marriage could be. I truly believed it was our best year.

So how could we go from the best of times to Ron's downfall. The old song by Cinderella: "…you don't know what you've got, till it's gone…" makes me think of the opposite of that; "you don't know what you're missing till you get it." The "good feeling" of nurturing from another woman was what Ron succumbed to because it was absent in our relationship.

Ron fell into the "good feeling" of being nurtured. This feeling deceived him into thinking it was okay to allow someone into his personal space, the intimate space of emotional and physical affection.

Ron was facing some pretty big giants at the time, and I wasn't emotionally there for him, simply because I didn't know how. Please understand this is why REVEAL is so important—because many of us have no idea HOW to be emotionally available for each other in our relationships.

It can be so easy to retrieve and hide behind the rock wall all the while justifying needing a little relief or comfort in your down times. For many, it may be the rocks of alcohol, drugs, food, shopping, or sexual addiction that you fall back on when you are looking for relief. For Ron, life had spun out of control as he faced his mother's death and as our business exploded with success. Yes, I said success. Ron's fear of success brought him to a new all-time low of inadequacy.

Sometimes we are so blinded by our pain that we even believe God has sent us a "friend" (or a coping mechanism with skin on) to help us through. Unfortunately, once the friendship goes from reality to what we call a "feel good" trance, you are heading for an affair and in big trouble. This is why today, Ron says if it begins to feel good, it's wrong and you'd better run. This kind of intimacy is to be reserved for your spouse alone. If you don't share this with them, it's time to start the road towards recovery through revealing, so when you face the inevitable giants of life, you face them together as a couple.

Unfortunately for us, facing the giants together came after Ron's infidelity, but if our story can help you avoid causing each other and your family more pain, then our story has been redeemed.

I had to ask myself some brutal questions after the affair. I believe everyone facing infidelity today or in the past should ask these same questions. The questions I posed to myself were the beginning of my healing as I was determined to not being a victim. So here is what I asked myself: "What part did I play in the infidelity? Where was I when our lives were falling apart? (See the truth was, dear reader, I was so busy building this awesome business and ministry, I was oblivious to what was going on around me).

Well, God didn't take long to reveal the truth since I asked. God is good and He does not turn us away when we are broken. As I asked the questions, my heart was breaking but I was desperate and I needed to know how this could've happened. I remembered the verse in the Bible I'd heard preached so many times. It was a verse I'd memorized and now I needed to hang on to it like never before. I want to share it with you because if today you are broken then I plead with you to offer God the sacrifice of your broken heart. Look at what it says in Psalm 51:17(NIV) "My sacrifice, O God, is a broken spirit; a broken and contrite heart you, God, will not despise."

God was faithful and took me back (the REVEAL journey) to when I was twenty-three-years-old, a friend (only a few years older) whom I loved very much died of cancer. I remember so clearly I was invited by his family to the viewing of the body and it was there I placed a red rose on his chest and while saying my last goodbye I found myself vowing to never love like that again.

When I asked God with a contrite heart what had I done, Jesus gave me a vision of the rose I had laid in the casket. I did a double take as I saw the rose was still alive nineteen years later. I heard that familiar small, still voice of God tell me to pick up the rose and break the vow I had made to never love like that again.

I had withheld a nurturing heart from my husband and children. Because I had cared for and nurtured my friend through one year of illness, the part of me to nurture was buried with him. It was the beginning of January 1998, that God revealed to me the part I played in Ron's infidelity. He showed me that in breaking the vow I would get my whole heart back. In obedience to the revelation, I can truly say my husband and children have my whole heart. Today I choose to nurture because I will never let the enemy gain that foothold again in my life.

The potential destruction of our marriage was another way, I believe, the enemy of our faith tried to take us out. But the laugh is on him, because once we decided to restore our relationship, our story has become a great source of healing to thousands of others facing the same devastation. Again, the giant eraser I spoke of earlier was not going to be used, not even on this story.

Please know that intimacy takes time and safety and trust to build. It also takes revealing the heart and acknowledging the dark and wounded places. Our hearts long for intimacy, but all too often the rocks we carry into the relationship with us rob us of the joy we were meant to share as a couple.

———

I like what Julie Sibert from Intimacy in Marriage said in her blog, "As Christians, we have no excuse for not learning all we can about having great marriages, including great sex. So stop letting modesty destroy your sexual intimacy. No one at the PTA knows what you're doing beneath the sheets. Live fully as if you know that to be the truth."

If we are talking about revealing our sexual beliefs, we will once again need to go back to what we saw, heard, and experienced in our own homes. If you think back to the home you were raised in, was there affection? Was the topic of sex taboo? Were you raised in a religious home and the only thing you heard about sex was, "don't do it"?

If you were to make a list of negative thoughts when it comes to sex, what would they be? How do you think these thoughts affect your intimacy? If you had to REVEAL your past when it comes to the subject of sex, would your storyboard have a lot of regrets or painful memories? Was there sexual abuse? Were you exposed to pornography? What does your past REVEAL about your sexual belief system? If you are a Christian woman, you may believe modesty is to be carried out not only out of the bedroom but also in the bedroom. This is not the truth, although you may believe it.

Intimacy is one of those words that again can be taken in so many directions depending on your experience or lack of experience with it. I once heard it put like this; IN-TO-ME-SEE. If we can make that our standard, how well

LOVE, SEX AND MONEY

does your spouse know you? How deep have you let them in, or are there still secrets that have not been revealed between the two of you.

Now in saying that, here is the ugly side of this word and it only shows up as that if we use it against each other. Because intimacy is so private, so deep, so personal, it should be treated as a gem given to you by your partner. Unfortunately, when the tide turns, and anger and resentment build up and separation or divorce is on the table as an option to solve your problems, sometimes those intimate moments that were the pinnacle of your relationship, the time you felt the closest, can now be turned into grenades that are tossed back at you and sometimes be made public. How sad. How dishonoring to each other. This is partially the reason why divorce is so devastating.

Has this happened to you or do you know someone it has happened to? It is devastating and will definitely increase the rocks in that strong wall of defense, which now maybe a fortress for some of you dear readers. This will not only kill intimacy in present relationships but also future ones, even if divorce is not involved—when our intimate moments are shared without permission, it is devastating.

We believe our secrets keep us sick. That doesn't mean that we are meant to go and share all our secrets of shame and guilt with everyone, but it does mean you can't keep them inside. The Bible talks about confessing your wrongs to one another. Why is that? It's because God created us to have healthy emotions to enjoy an abundant life, and when we have shame and guilt inside we get clogged up. Our heart, medically speaking now, will not tolerate toxic emotions for long before we begin to get physically sick. This goes for your sex life as well. Secrets from your past regarding sexuality will inhibit you and keep the intimacy in the bedroom sick.

So the first step, once again, is to REVEAL the truth. We suggest you be vulnerable with yourself. What do we mean by that? Start by creating a safe place for yourself, somewhere where you know you will not be interrupted, and create a story board of what you saw, heard, and experienced around sex in your younger years. What were you exposed to emotionally, physically, and spiritually regarding intimacy and sex?

Now comes the hard part: start revealing if anything inappropriate happened to you as the victim, or maybe you were the one who actually hurt someone sexually. It all needs to be confessed, and maybe right now you can only confess it to God. That works because there is no one safer than Jesus when it comes to our shame. And take comfort that He already knows; He was there then and He is here now. Just remind yourself that secrets keep you sick, and those secrets have probably already robbed you of some pretty good years, both in your personal life, and if you are married, in your intimacy.

–Tina

I remember when I was first willing to start the journey of REVEAL and disclose what was in my heart; what I discovered was a surprise to me. Like I mentioned before, Ron and I had good sex and since neither of us had sexual relations prior to marriage, we grew in that area together. Now, when I say I had never had prior sexual relations, I mean outside of my sexual abuse, which involved intercourse twice when I was a young teen. Overall, we were both pretty pure. I would advocate for purity all day long, because as a woman I did not have to worry about being compared to others, and I needed that reassurance. I had enough feelings of not being good enough for him; at least those feelings of inadequacy were not in the bedroom. So, our sexual activity was pretty experimental and for the most part really good, but there was a time before marriage that I had fear of entering marriage with a virgin man.

I remember the first time I confessed my fear to a couple of friends. It was our first week back in college. I call them intimate friends because of what I dared to share with them. We had finished our second year of college, and that summer they were married. So, in our third year of college, they lived in the married quarters and one night they invited me for dinner. One conversation led to another and finally I asked the question, how is sex? They could see I wasn't joking. They both answered "good," but my girlfriend answered, "Sometimes, I have trouble getting the images of other girls he's been with out of my mind." She was a virgin when she married and felt very ripped off that she saved herself for him and he had not. That night in my friend's apartment I received healing. It's amazing to me how God will take a normal young woman's inquisitive conversation and turn into a healing moment.

The reason I had asked the question was because deep inside of me laid a fear that was based on what I had heard back when I was fourteen years old at my parents' business.

They owned a small hotel in downtown Vancouver. I would spend the summer cleaning rooms and working in the office. One day, I met a young Amish couple on their honeymoon and I remember them being very friendly, and they would often stop and talk to me. One morning I knocked on their door to clean their room and there was no answer to my knock. So I opened the door and saw her lying there crying. I said sorry and went to close the door. She said, "No, come in," so I entered and sat on the bed. I asked her the obvious, "What is wrong?" She told me the story of the night before; they had both individually gone and hired hookers. She had gone and found a male hooker and was now lying there feeling sick. She explained that they had tried to have sex and it wasn't working. My fourteen-year-old mind could not process this, and a seed was planted inside of me that marrying a virgin was not desirable. That night at my friend's apartment, I let my secret out and began the process of rewriting my story that really was based on their story of sexual failure. Just because the couple years before were damaged by how they grew up and viewed sex in their Amish community did not mean I had to be afraid of marrying a virgin. Had I not revealed my past with my friends and rewritten (by seeing it from a different perspective, my girlfriend's perspective—she battled images of other women with her husband) my story, I would have gone into marriage carrying the fear of a fourteen year old.

Another big REVEAL came when I went through the five-day intensive program back in 1993. The area of sexual damage came up, and I remember Ron asking me if the reason I didn't like touching him sexually was because of my abusers. It was like a light bulb clicked on, and I realized every one of my abusers made me touch him that way. Again, another healing from revealing the past, although I did not recognize the connection prior to the question being asked. I tell you this not to reveal my personal stuff but hopefully to help you ask yourself some difficult but essential questions.

Sex was God's design, not only for procreation but also for comfort and pleasure between a husband and wife. The Bible tells us not to withhold it from each other, so that tells me its sole purpose is more than just making babies. The Bible goes on to say that if you withhold sex from your spouse, you leave yourself open for temptation. Now, withholding might mean a lot more than intercourse; I believe God is talking about sharing our personal space or intimacy with each other.

If you are not married, then pursue healing so that your friendships can be healthy and you too can enjoy intimate, non-sexual relationships before marriage.

As individuals you will also have to REWRITE and RENEW your story. This will avert disaster in any present or future relationship.

But while we are still in the REVEAL stage, I encourage you to follow Ron's instructions at the end of this chapter and create your personal Storyboard. Find a quite safe environment where you will not be interrupted during this exercise.

This is not going to be an easy process but the healing far outweighs the discomfort.

We continue to experience couples being destroyed and heading to divorce courts in droves because the REVEAL process has not taken place. Once couples begin to acknowledge what has brought them to these relational roadblocks, healing can begin. So as you gain knowledge from your Storyboard, use it to grow, but more importantly, use it to heal.

How to REVEAL

All of these stories we have shared with you lead us to the place of HONESTY where we can discover who we are and why we believe what we do.

Now it's your turn. It's time to REVEAL your past.

Start by making your own Storyboard. You will need a large poster board (any paper size will do if you do not have poster board) and a couple of felt pens. Draw a horizontal line through the middle of the board.

Above the line, identify the positive moments in your life. It might be goals accomplished, people and relationships that influenced you, college, marriage, a career, birth of a child etc.

Below the line, identify the negative events that shaped you. An event can be big or small, but if it left a negative mark on your emotions; make sure to identify it.

When you are done, go through your storyboard and pick out the top three painful experiences or events that still sting when you remember them.

These are the stories you will want to share and process with someone, and dig deeper into. Let them guide and comfort you as you mourn and move towards letting go, forgiving, and healing from the wounds affecting your present.

These are the stories impacting your behavior today!

Think back on how you dealt with the pain. Have you forgiven the perpetrator? Are you able to forgive yourself? Are you still blaming God or someone else?

Consider attending a four day intensive Relationship Lifeline or maybe reaching out to one of our Coaches to help you REVEAL life's hurts for the sake of healing and resolving the past.

CHAPTER 9

REWRITE - BLAME TO FORGIVENESS

"Resentment is like drinking poison and then hoping it will kill your enemies." – Nelson Mandela

–Ron

There are three elements to rewriting our story. The first is deciding this is the course of action you want to take. The second, and I believe the most crucial, is to see through the eyes of compassion. And third is to allow yourself the gift of forgiveness.

–Tina

For more than half my life, I struggled to come to terms with my mother's inability to accept me. Her words "you should not have been born" haunted me. I developed death fantasies as a result of her words. I felt that if I shouldn't have been born then I should just die. It was a fatalistic mentality, and it kept me from truly allowing contentment in my life. I felt incredible anger towards her and blamed her for everything that hurt me. After all, if I shouldn't have been born, then she should not have given birth to me in the first place. She brought me into this world so it was all her fault.

I will never forget the first time I really understood the work of compassion and forgiveness. It was at the five-day program in 1993. The instructor led us in an experiential exercise of forgiveness. We were instructed to think of someone we needed to forgive who had done something to us that was "unforgivable." When prompted to participate in the exercise, I instantly knew who I should focus my attention on, but my heart was so hardened against my mother I tried to think of another candidate—someone easier to forgive and have compassion for.

However, my mind remained locked on her. Reluctantly, I took the first step and made the decision to forgive the woman, only two years before in the counselor's office, I had refused to talk about. I closed my eyes and took a couple of forced deep breaths. I tried to picture my mother as vulnerable, which was difficult to do while picturing her as an adult. It took seeing her as a child to make the mental switch. I let my imagination take me to that little town in Southern Italy where she was born. I saw her in the distance standing in front of a house. As I walked closer, I could see that she had the frame of a seven or eight-year-old girl. Her head was hanging down so her hair shadowed her face, and her shoulders were rising up and down in a syncopated rhythm. As I walked closer I heard sounds from inside the house that led me to believe she was outside looking for safety. It was then I looked at her and my gaze remained locked on her eyes. Her eyes were framed with tears as she sobbed, and the light in them exuded a forlorn and lonely spirit almost like a candle that flickers before being blown out. I could look deep into those eyes and see straight into her broken heart, bruised from the beatings of responsibilities that should have never been hers. I realized that I had been so engrossed in my own pain that I never acknowledged her hardships of growing up. At that moment what I heard, saw and experienced changed everything. Immediately compassion filled my heart.

Every time I blinked, my mother's desolate gaze reemerged. As I was trying to chase away the image, I heard the whisper of a gentle small voice, "Tina, those aren't only your mother's eyes, they're yours too." I lurched forward in my seat and buried my face in my hands as I began sobbing audibly. The awareness that my mother and I were linked by a common thread of loneliness and rejection hit me and led me to another insight. The eyes that my mother and I shared were the same eyes that had haunted me for over two years. They were the reason for the eighty-pound weight gain, the shame of the hypocrisy while I taught God's love to children and the resentment I harbored for the counselor. The eyes I saw past my mothers eyes and my eyes were the eyes we gave up the Hawaiian vacation for. The eyes were my precious baby girl's eyes. In that moment of revelation that we were all linked by a generational cord of rejection, unexpectedly and miraculously, the rejection I had held for Jenny disappeared. No amount of preaching or teaching could have prepared me for the freedom I felt in that one single moment. When all the dots connected and I truly went from my head, where the toxic thoughts had tried to destroy me, to my heart, where the yearning for real love had alluded me for over thirty years. Dear reader, I have no words to describe the feeling or the emotion of that moment, but I can tell you the moment became moments, hours, days and now years. I promised myself while I took the last step of rewriting, forgiveness, I would never look back. I received the gift that day and I could have gone home and my life would've changed forever and my money would have been well spent. Imagine though we were only at the end of day two. There was so much more to rewriting and renewing and I was ready for it.

–Ron

Forgiveness is the third level to REWRITE. People often wonder if forgiveness requires them to forget the transgressions of the person who hurt them. We don't believe you can forgive and forget and even if forgetting was possible it is not beneficial to you. Forgetting would deprive you of the lessons you learned or the strength you gained from the pain you experienced. Forgiveness is for your own freedom so you do not have to carry the weight of the rocks of rejection, anger, resentment, and rebellion in your heart. Forgiveness saves you from rotting from the inside out. Forgiveness does not condone an offense or excuse the transgressor. You can forgive someone that has already passed away or forgive an offense without any promise of restoration. Making the decision to forgive doesn't guarantee that you won't get hurt again nor that you shouldn't set healthy boundaries in abusive relationships.

> *Forgiving does not erase the bitter past. A healed memory is not a deleted memory. Instead, forgiving what we cannot forget creates a new way to remember. We change the memory of our past into a hope for our future. –Lewis B. Smedes*

–Tina

When I applied forgiveness to my own story, I learned that the only power I had was the power to change me. By completing the inner work, I was finally able to REWRITE the words that had hurt me for so long. Remember the statement, "You should have never been born." Now listen as I apply the REWRITE principle; "You should have never been born, NOW." That one shift in perspective, that one word "NOW" changed the whole meaning of what I had heard for years. Remember the sixteen year old girl I saw on my Storyboard? The same eight year old standing outside her home, scared and looking for a place of safety, here she was just a few years later with the chance to be free. The freedom she was looking for did not last long. Barely a few weeks after her honeymoon she was pregnant with me. Timing was her source of pain. Without forgiveness I would have never been able to REWRITE that story that plagued for as long as I'd heard and registered those once fatalistic words.

–Ron

I want to share a study with you, from the Institute of Heart Math, on the physical impact forgiveness has on your DNA. We aren't just telling you to forgive because we think it's a good idea. You have the power to change your generational legacy by rewriting your thoughts.

What kind of legacy will you leave—a generational curse or a blessing?

Local and Non-Local Effects of Coherent Heart Frequencies on Conformational Changes of DNA3

Human placenta DNA (the most pristine form of DNA) was placed in a container from which they could measure changes in the DNA. Twenty-eight vials of DNA were given (one each) to 28 trained researchers. Each researcher had been trained how to generate and FEEL feelings, and they each had strong emotions. What was discovered was that the DNA CHANGED ITS SHAPE according to the feelings of the researchers:

When the researchers FELT gratitude, love, and appreciation, the DNA responded by RELAXING and the strands unwound. The length of the DNA became longer.

When the researchers FELT anger, fear, frustration, or stress, the DNA responded by TIGHTENING UP. It became shorter and SWITCHED OFF many of our DNA codes. The shutdown of the DNA codes was reversed and the codes were switched back on again when feelings of love, joy, gratitude and appreciation were felt by the researchers.

What this research concludes is that un-forgiveness and toxic thoughts physically alter your DNA.

CHAPTER 10

REWRITE - CANCER

"The thief comes only to steal and kill and destroy; I have come that they may have life, and have it to the full." John 10:10 (NIV)

–Tina

Ron and I had spent nearly a decade traveling and helping people across North America confront their fears and unresolved issues by the time December 5th, 2009 rolled around. It was a Thursday in Irvine, California, and we were just beginning yet another intensive Relationship Lifeline. Before our dinner break, I pulled out my phone and noticed three missed calls from my mother. I immediately called her back as I had heard the urgency of her voice in her messages and braced myself for the news. A thousand thoughts ran through my head of what could be wrong. Were my children alright? My mom and my adult children reside in Vancouver, BC. Had there been an accident? However, I was completely unprepared for the actual news. My mother had an urgent tone as she explained to me that we needed to call Ron's doctor.

On the first day of December, Ron had gone to the Emergency room of the Burnaby General Hospital in Vancouver, BC to have a mole removed from his left thigh. It was a simple procedure and everything seemed fine. He had the mole looked at a few times by different doctors over the years and as they examined it and asked a couple of questions, they assured Ron it really didn't look like anything.

–Ron

As we dialed our voice-mail to hear the doctor's message, the doctor's voice seemed to echo against my skull as he said, "Ron, this is Dr. Silverthorne, your results came back from pathology and it is life threatening. I suggest you come home immediately." The words hit me like a brick. My lungs collapsed and refused to take in air. I couldn't breathe. I slowly looked towards Tina, who had also just heard the news. All the color drained from our faces, but we remained stoic. Part of me felt as if it was a bad dream, but the reality set in as we received subsequent phone calls from our children. The doctor had called Tina's mom as he could not reach us and did not have a California number on file. Tina's mother discerned urgency in the doctor's voice and failing to reach us on the phone, she called our children.

Though I was shocked at this new turn of events in my life, I maintained my focus. We looked at each other and silently agreed to keep our composure for the sake of our team and our attendees. We knew what this weekend meant to the people there. Knowing that each of those families was in crisis too. We couldn't bring ourselves to abandon them.

It wasn't until we returned to our hotel room, late in the evening, that we let our guard down. Our children begged us to return to Vancouver on the earliest flight possible. We were all emotional as a family, and even though there was distance between us, we could hear the desperate cry in our children's voices. We needed each other's support to cope with this unexpected news, but our heart was here also with the couples in the Relationship Lifeline. After talking and discussing between ourselves, Tina and I chose to stay and complete the seminar. Our good friend Stan was with us that weekend as a volunteer trainer. We confided in him as he was a nurse at one of the best cancer clinics in Northern California. He was able to calm our spirits and also spoke with our children over the phone. His advice was, "Going home immediately was not necessary other than for the reason of getting the family together. Stan said, "The good news is you are not going to die this weekend."

Sunday evening, our work was done and Tina and I began packing to return home. At one point, we both paused and looked intently into each other's eyes. I studied the woman I loved, and admired her fortitude. Even though I knew how anxious she was to get home, she seemed so calm, unlike the woman I had known in the past.

–Tina

I felt a weird peace but it came in waves. There were times that inside I was screaming and crying and banging at the walls. I wanted to be able to do something. I wanted, with every piece of me, to make the diagnosis go away. At that moment fretting for what was about to un-fold I longed for the GIANT ERASER.

My gaze remained on Ron's eyes and that seemed to anchor me. I knew we were going to have to come to grips with our new reality. We were going to have to apply every lesson we had ever learned and every teaching we had ever taught. Were we going to focus on the disease or were we going to focus on our destiny? Our God given assignment was to heal the broken hearted and we both knew we were not done. The thief wanted to take us out, and this was not a new thing, as he had tried so many times before. His attempt to destroy our marriage, steal our finances, and now he was back to kill with this new diagnosis. Thank God for Jesus as He came to give us life and that to the fullest.

With this new turn of events FAITH was going to take a front seat. Though FEAR lingered we would not allow it to overtake us. The good news is we never lost one night's sleep. I realized that when you give up your old friends like CONTROL and ANGER, which are fueled by fear, you have to replace them with new friends. I learned this lesson early in the REWRITE of my story. I asked FAITH and PEACE to be my friends during this fearful journey.

We were in the eye of the storm. As soon as we returned home, we were bombarded with more news from doctors telling us that there was no treatment, no cure, and no hope—only four to twelve months to live. Despite how far I had come with all my inner work, I could feel myself slipping. I had to draw on my faith and peace so as not to slip below the line where FEAR dwelled.

Like the apostle Paul there were times I did not know if I was having an in or out of body experience as I watched Faith & Fear war one with another.

The first Sunday, after returning from Vancouver, Ron got up early to get ready for church. I remained in bed and pulled the covers up around me. I had no desire to go to church. I didn't have the energy. I wanted to hide under the covers and bury my face in the pillow. I silently begged God for anything to help ease the pain. "God, please give me peace. Tell me he isn't going to die." I closed my eyes and a stream of tears began to dampen my pillow.

I had to find a way to REWRITE this story. In the blink of an eye I saw a tombstone and on it I saw Ron's birthdate and the dash–only to hear God asking me, "Child, do you believe that I determined before his birth the day he would be born and even the day he would die?" With reluctance, I said "YES." As I surrendered my will, the peace came.

Dear reader at the time of writing this book, Ron and I have been through a journey of PEACE but not without a fight. We are now nearly at the four year mark since the diagnosis. Our Storyboard has new highs and lows. The latest diagnosis came July 19, 2013 when again we sat in the same doctor's office with the same doctor saying, "It looks like the cancer is back in several organs. We really have nothing we can offer you and, at best, you have several months."

My very best friend FAITH rose up within me and uttered as quickly as the doctors words came out, "OR NOT, were these not the same words spoken nearly four years ago?" The doctor's head pointed to the ground, and I wondered how many times these poor doctors look at the tiled floor as they must speak words of death. But here FAITH could do no other than speak up. I continued speaking, "One thing we know and that is that God determines the day you are born and only He determines the day we will die, and we are totally okay with that."

His PEACE filled the room and our daughter Jenny, who was with us, looked up, dried her tears, and both the doctor and the nurse looked up from the floor, nodded their heads and sat there in agreement with us. We all smiled as we left the doctor's office.

Dear friend, if today you are going through a challenge, stop and listen to what is going through your head. Listen to the thoughts and the voices. Are they based in love or fear? Love conquers all, but you have to let it.

So I ask you again, "What is love?"

CHAPTER 11

REWRITE - PLOWED UP

"It is not a question of God allowing or not allowing things to happen. It is a part of living. Some things we do to ourselves, other things we do to each other. Our Father knows about every bird, which falls to the ground, but he does not always prevent it from falling. What are we to learn from this? It is that our response to what happens is more important than what happens. Here is a mystery: one man's experience drives him to curse God, while another man's identical experience drives him to bless God. Your response to what happens is more important than what happens." - Chip Brogden

–Ron

It was in October of 2011 when Tina and I traveled to Germany to receive treatment for the incurable melanoma I had been diagnosed with two years earlier. One morning, in between treatments, I was out walking along the perimeter of the little town of Nidda. I meandered through several farmer's fields. A farmer on his tractor caught my eye as he plowed his field. Now if you're not a farmer, I will do my best to describe this so you get a better picture.

On the back of the tractor was a plow. It has a sharp edge that slices deep into the ground and flips the soil hidden underneath to the top to expose it to the air and light. It doesn't look pretty. In fact it looks a mess. If you didn't know the process, you would think, "How could anything good grow there?"

The idea of plowing is to expose the older soil and to give it new life. Even though it has been hidden for a long time, there is good ground underneath that needs to be cultivated so the field can produce an excellent crop. If the farmer simply relies on the surface soil or the top soil, it will eventually run out of nutrients, even though it looks fine and pretty. If you stay only on the surface level, the crop the soil produces is substandard and the true potential of that field is never realized.

I think you know where I am going here. If you would allow me, I am going to take a small excerpt from the piece I wrote to my family and close friends who were sending me e-mails and prayers every day while I was in Germany. This was written a few days after my seven hour surgery.

To put this week into perspective for me has been somewhat difficult. I knew this surgery and Chemo infusion into my leg was going to be big, but the doctors never really give you the full picture nor prepare you. I have never experienced such agonizing physical pain. Spiritually speaking, God has really been doing His own surgery on me this week. This week has felt like I have been plowed up. Every second year, the farmer "plows" with the big gnarly curved sharp piece of metal that digs deep into the ground. It turns everything over from the depths and brings it to the surface, the light and the air exposes everything.... I am such a mess. That is all I can say. I look pretty good on the outside, but under that nice soil is some pretty messed up stuff. I know experiences like this are for His glory, whatever the outcome. I don't want to miss that. My prayer for you today, my family and friends is to allow yourself to get "plowed up" a little. Allow healing to take place under that good looking soil. HE is our healer emotionally, physically and spiritually but healing only takes place after something has been exposed. Ouch!

In Ephesians, Chapter 5 it talks about how we came out of the darkness and into the Light of the Lord. It instructs us to walk as children of that light through the fruit of the spirit. This is part of rewriting our life story.

Our lives are much like that farmer's field. We can keep it looking pretty, like nothing is wrong. When people pass by they admire you and tell you what a beautiful life and what an amazing marriage you have, but underneath where no one can see, is the stuff. Hopefully you were challenged enough from the last few chapters you have read, that you have begun to REVEAL and started your own Storyboard process.

I think it is pretty obvious to most of us that just revealing does not constitute healing. Just like the farmer and his field, he doesn't stop at plowing. He must cultivate the soil readying for new growth.

After we go through the pain of exposing everything, as we did in the previous chapters the next steps are to REWRITE and RENEW.

It is the process of changing your story from that of being a victim; keeping things buried, to becoming a victor; and using your new story as a gift to share. We cannot change what has happened in the past. We can however change how we feel about what happened in the past. This is the switch that will turn the lights on to your freedom!

How we feel about someone or something will always win over our intellect. Kerry Patterson said it best, "… when emotions run high, intelligence runs low…." You know intellectually forgiving an offence is the right thing to do. Unfortunately, our feelings get in the way, and until we can change those, the battle is almost impossible to win. I believe the fight is to come to the place where I want to forgive. The decision to confront the past and let it go is much more difficult than forgiveness.

Letting go of the past my friend, takes a determined willingness to let go of all of the blame, pointing fingers, denial, and anything else that might hinder you.

Chapter 12

Rewrite - Compassion

*And yet I will show you the most excellent way.
If I speak in the tongues of men or of angels,
but do not have love, I am only a resounding
gong or a clanging cymbal." 1 Corinthians
12:31 – 13:1 (NIV)*

–Ron

There are three elements to rewriting our story. The first is the DECISION on which course of action you want to take. The second, and I believe the most crucial, is to see through the eyes of COMPASSION, and thirdly is to give yourself the gift of FORGIVENESS.

Decision

I'm not going to take a lot of time on this one. God gave everyone on this earth a supernatural power. It's called the power of decision. It started with Adam and Eve, and it still is our greatest asset as well as our greatest liability.

Either you want to change or you don't. If you don't no need to read any further. When you are ready pick up this book again, I will lead you through it, or better yet attend one of our four day Relationship Lifelines' and we will walk you through the R3 FACTOR.

"Well, that's kind of harsh Ron!" Yes it is, but my response comes from pain—the pain of hearing countless people and especially Christians say, "Yup, I've forgiven my father, mother, ex-husband, ex-wife, abuser, rapist (or whomever)," and yet they still hold resentment, anger, and bitterness towards that person or people. While they said the words, and their *intention* was good, it didn't stick. Certainly they wanted to forgive—their mind was willing— but their feelings won over their intellect. The *rocks* got in the way, and forgiveness became an exercise of words, not a real change in their heart.

Compassion & Forgiveness

Dr. Steven Stosny writes in his book "*Compassion Power*" even the most hardened criminal can be led to show compassion. Tina and I attended his *Compassion Workshop* a number of years ago and deeply connected with the idea that we all have the ability to operate in compassion. Dr. Stosny worked within the prison system and proved that all men have the capacity to feel the pain of someone else, to walk a few steps in their shoes, and to connect emotionally with another person.

Isn't that what Jesus did as He hung on the cross? Even though He was in excruciating physical pain, emotionally spent, and felt spiritually abandoned by His own father, He still chose compassion. He offered the two thieves redemption and asked His Father to forgive those that crucified Him. It was his first act of intercession for us as sinners. He was not taking any malice, bitterness, anger or resentment with Him.

These final words are significant. He could have simply said, "Father forgive them" and left it at that. But it's almost like He makes an excuse for them. Those last few words in His statement let them off the hook! "They don't know what they are doing!" This is where compassion walks alongside forgiveness. Jesus saw into their hearts, and these words were the beginning of the compassionate grace we now live in today.

As you read this, I hope your heart is open to receiving Christ's love, maybe for the first time. If you are a believer think of what His love is still doing for you. It was through His compassion that He healed the sick and is still healing the wounded today!

CHAPTER 13

RENEW

But now you must also rid yourselves of all such things as these: anger, rage, malice, slander, and filthy language from your lips. Do not lie to each other, since you have taken off your old self with its practices and have put on the new self, which is being RENEWED in knowledge in the image of its Creator. Colossians 3:8-10 (NIV)

–Ron

Can you think of a time when you were either in a renovation or have seen a renovation and the thought crossed your mind, "How in the world are we/

they ever going to put all this back together? It's such a mess! This is going to take forever to rebuild." This is what you might be experiencing, or have experienced in the past when going through your own REVEAL. Your nice little house, you were so cozy in, just got rattled and shaken and ripped apart. When you decide you want to expand your living space or life, and live in more freedom, there is going to be some pain associated along with the renovation.

RENEW is about the rebuilding process. RENEW is about living out what we have learned through the REVEAL and REWRITE exercises. As we continue to restructure our belief systems, to be in line with "truth," God's truth, we are redefining every other unhealthy belief which does not line up with God's Word. Challenging the lies we have adopted –especially from our childhood can take a short time for some and a longer time for others.

What does Renewal look like?

Philippians 4:8 (NIV), *"Finally, brothers and sisters, whatever is true, whatever is noble, whatever is right, whatever is pure, whatever is lovely, whatever is admirable – if anything is excellent or praise worthy – think about such things."*

The daily practice of this scripture will surely set you on the path of renewal. Renewal must be a daily practice as human nature has the tendency to revert back to our old destructive ways.

–Tina

When it came to my husband's infidelity, my natural human tendencies would have been to take my Biblical right to divorce my husband for adultery and I suppose nobody would have blamed me. Yet, I was determined that if he was willing to restore our marriage, I was in. This was one of those gifts that my dad gave me. I knew I was my father's daughter when I took to heart his beliefs about fighting for family and divorce never being an option. He always used to say, "Families stick together no matter what. There's nothing that is so bad that you can't work it out and stay together."

To take your relationship to the next level commit to **REVEAL** your past, **REWRITE** your stories, and **RENEW** your minds.

CHAPTER 14

THE CHALLENGE

"During the first half of a marathon, I feel strong and fast and inspired. I'm having fun. Much later, after I pass the 20-mile mark and I'm no longer having fun, I start telling myself that I'm in the homestretch. Past the 23-mile mark, hey, it's only a 5K race. But the miles between 13 and 20, the "in between" miles, are the most mentally challenging." Ryan Hall

(Posted in 2013 Boston Marathon, Athlete Spotlight)

–Ron

Challenge:

It is not difficult to surmise the picture of the marathon runner and our relationships. It is just what life is. There are going to be fun then dry spells, and loveless times when you just feel like packing it in. It's just not worth it. There is a saying I heard years ago; "When the pain of staying is greater than the pain of leaving, then leave." You read Shannon Tweed Simmons' quote earlier in the book about loosing your right to leave when you get married and have kids. So why has it become more of the norm now, to leave? People don't know about the 17 or 18 or 20 mile marker. They weren't expecting that uphill climb, the wet weather, the unexpected fall or two. There is a point where you have to dig deep, and not go by your feelings but by what the truth is. When we are at our lowest point all we have is the truth that will lead us to freedom.

So, that is my challenge. We have given you some tools in this book. Don't give up on yourself or your family. If the other person will not participate in the growth needed, then grow for yourself and if you have children, for them.

Be the best mom or dad you can be, with or without your partner! Step out and become the person God intended you to be, on the inside first.

Jesus promised an abundant life here on Earth, not just in Heaven. We are rightful heirs to the inheritance of peace, fulfillment, security, joy, healing, and love. Although we are a work in progress, we can honestly say we're happy with the journey God has led us on. We have a beautiful family. We've been through a lot together, but our trials and tribulations have drawn us closer together.

We ask you to find the courage to start renewing your mind, heart, and spirit. Look deep into your past and don't back down from the pain you find there. Confront it and all the fear that comes attached to it. Confront it with an embrace.

Thank God for the truth that sets us free. We believe with all our heart the words of the prophet Isaiah:

Isaiah 40: 29-31 (NIV)

He gives strength to the weary and increases the power of the weak. Even youths grow tired and weary, and young men stumble and fall; but those who hope in the Lord will RENEW their strength. They will soar on wings like eagles;

they will run and not grow weary, they will walk and not be faint.

Dare to Live Above the Line, face your REALITY and start the R3 FACTOR journey today.

TESTIMONIALS

Dear Reader,

As I prepared and edited Ron's and my book for our second printing, I thought about how 3 years have now passed since Ron left my side to go and be with his creator on December 25, 2013. As his wife of 32 years, I believe and take comfort that Ron died in faith not seeing the promises all fulfilled but he sees us carry on in that great cloud of witness. I reread the book and marveled that not much has changed except the name of our 4 day seminar. The same passion that the both of us had when we started the venture of healing the brokenhearted remains today! God continues to propel me and my staff towards that same end. It is without hesitation that I say that these stories in the testimonial section of the first printing are the precise reason why Ron's legacy and my passion remains strong and steadfast today as it was 20 years ago. These stories are found along with many others on our web site;

www.relationshiplifeline.org .

We are fortunate to stay in contact with many of our couples who share their success that continues after seminar. Josh and Jamie Hubbert took the R3 Principles to heart after attending our seminar. They use the principles in their daily lives. The Hubbert's came to Lifeline in financial ruin, broken trust and no hope that their marriage was salvageable. Today 8 years later they have rebuilt their finances, their trust and their children have a mom and dad who have stood the test of time and are together to live life with them. One of our taglines

"WE GET TO" has a special place in the Hubbert's life.

With every success it should be noted that Ron and I would pray for our lifeline attendees without ceasing those 4 days. God's grace and sovereignty reigns strong. Our 4 Day Intensives are non religious and no one is excluded because of their beliefs systems. This being said I continue to uphold the promise of looking to God for strength, stamina and wisdom as myself and my staff run our seminars.

CHAPTER 15

"HOME IS WHERE OUR STORY BEGINS"

...Relationship Lifeline Graduates
Their complete stories along, with many others can be found at www.RelationshipLifeline.org

<u>Chris and Dawn Lewis – I Don't Love You Anymore</u>

In July of 2009, as we packed to go to a July 4th pool party, my husband announced to me, "I don't love you. I don't think I have ever loved you." After thirteen years of marriage and three children, this was the reality I now had to deal with. What do you do when your life comes crashing down?

But how to tell the children? What do you tell the children? When? Where? While I was an adult and could take responsibility for my part in the failure of the marriage, the children were the victims of our failure. Chris was confident that over time the kids would adjust just fine and learn to embrace their new reality. I prayed for God to put our family back together.

One evening after about one month of separation, Quinn our young son was convinced that the separation was his fault. He knew that a lot of conflict in the house was usually triggered by something he said or did. We often disagreed on how to manage him or discipline him. The logical conclusion for a nine-year-old then was that the current problem must have been caused by him. While eating dinner one night, Quinn declared to me, "This is my entire fault. I caused dad to leave." He cried and sobbed, and there was absolutely nothing I could do or say to console him or convince him that he was wrong.

I just had to sit back and watch my children in pain with absolutely no remedy.

One day as I was taking Quinn to his football game, he asked a question that must have been haunting him for months. "Mom, is there any chance that you and dad will get back together?" I prayed to say the right words with honesty but tenderness. I had asked Chris the same question for the past six months, and his answer was always steadfast and firm: No. I knew I must not lie and I must speak from a place of truth. I answered, "No, Quinn. There is no chance that your father and I will get back together." However, no amount of time, no movie, no book, no therapy could have prepared me for his response. "Then I just want to die. I want to take a knife and stab myself in the stomach." And he sobbed. And I sobbed. My son was suicidal. My son wanted to die. All I could say was "I am sorry Quinn."

I confronted Chris and told him that the children were not okay. That he was wrong, and his choice to leave our family was destroying our children. He refused to believe me. However, the next evening, Chris called in tears. The reality of the situation—the fact that our children were wounded by his choices—began to sink in. He began to see the effects of his behavior on his children, and he felt lost.

A friend told me of a local Relationship Lifeline that we could attend. I was willing to do anything to put our family back together, but Chris had no intention of saving the marriage. He wanted to figure out how we could help the children through the pain of divorce. I suggested the

Lifeline to him as a way to give us the tools to communicate and help our children. He agreed to attend the four-day intensive workshop, while I prayed for a miracle.

In May 2009, after the first day of Lifeline—where Chris had missed the opening half due to work—I was convinced that he would not return for the remaining three days. He was confronted by Tina, and I thought for sure he would refuse to come back. However, the next morning Chris showed up. After several days of revealing and digging deep into our pasts, our resentments, our pain, our habits of mind, our motives and insecurities, we emerged to a new place where we could look at each other with new eyes, new perspectives, and new understanding. We began to rewrite by forgiving ourselves for our failures and mistakes and to forgive each other for the actions that led to the failure of our marriage. By the third night of the Relationship Lifeline, we had decided that we could work together to rebuild our marriage: to put the past behind us, to use the past as a stepping stone, and to move forward as one.

We sat down in the same den where six months earlier we had announced our separation. Now, we had joyous news of a miracle, we were ready to begin rewriting the chapters of our story.

We had moved to a place of forgiveness, but now began the work of renewing and never rebuilding that wall of rocks.

Josh & Jamie Hubbert – From Riches to Rags!

I had discovered that my husband had hid a lot of financial decisions he had made without me, which buried us in more debt and stress than I anticipated or could handle. He lied many times about our finances in a very weak attempt to save me from the truth and try and fix it on his own, but he could not. Trust was lost and we began to lose everything.

Our marriage was in jeopardy. I cannot even express how angry and bitter I had grown, not to mention lonely. I felt like my husband had damaged everything we had worked for. I questioned myself for a long time if I was even in love with him anymore and was terrified for our future.

Life in the past had always been good to me, and we had gone from riches to rags. Divorce could not be my future. I knew we needed to do something more drastic then counseling sessions and reading books. I tried to imagine how I would sit down and tell the boys that, "Mommy isn't happy anymore." It just seemed too selfish or unfair for me to disrupt their lives to the point of devastation.

Finally something new was introduced to us, a close friend led me to something called Relationship Lifeline, and I had no idea that calling Tina Konkin, that day would forever change my future.

When we walked into the conference ballroom, I was ready to unleash, I was full of anger and rage. My main plea was to fix my jerk of a husband. I had no idea what I was about to learn about me.

The following four days at Lifeline ended up being some of the best days of my adult life. Our marriage would be forever changed. It was no picnic; it was hard, challenging, and humbling. However at the same time, it was eye opening, encouraging and I saw and learned things like forgiveness and compassion for what seemed like the first time. Their way of taking us through the steps of the R3 Factor was amazing.

As I began to see things differently, think differently, and see my husband differently, the journey of rewriting began. We left Lifeline a different couple and different people. I could write paragraphs on what I learned, but needless to say the best thing that came out of Lifeline was how my husband and I began to renew and operate differently in our marriage.

The most important thing is that we had tools and Coaches available to us to walk along side of Josh and I when we got stuck!

The R3 Factor Tools:

1. Reveal what is going on inside when we hit walls.

2. Rewrite: To simply see things through different glasses and with compassion and forgiveness.

3. Renew by changing our programming.

Thank you Ron and Tina for your calling.

Mark

Ok Guys, this is "No longer left out" here to tell you a quick story...

So for me, this Relationship Lifeline was the most incredible thing that I have ever done. (Thirty-two rehabs in my day and dozens of independent counseling sessions along with 21 years of marriage dysfunction give me that credibility.) So many changes took place for me, that my life has already completely changed and there has already even been changes within the dynamics of my family.

So... Let me tell you...! Was it a heart attack? You be the judge!

I remember lying on my back. I remember holding up the rock representing all the hurt and shame that I received from my father as a child. In the midst I felt ready to let that go. But when Margaret spoke and said "are you ready to let it all   go, whatever is holding you back", 4 things came into my mind about 5 seconds apart. These thoughts floated through my mind in slow motion... It was my step-daughter, it was my mother I hadn't spoken to in 4 months, it was my blood daughter that I had not spoken to in 1 1/2 years and it was my oldest son whom I have had a completely broken relationship & have not spoken to in over a year. I wanted to let all this hurt and resentment go but felt that I was still hanging on to it just a little. I felt the exercise was to be over any minute so I decided just to drop the rock and maybe it would go away. Just as I dropped the rock, Paul put his hand on my heart for about 10 seconds (I assumed that he said a quick prayer for me, but I never heard him verbalize any words). Just then the exercise was over. I felt relief (at least in letting my daddy issues totally go). As I rolled gently to get up

I felt the worst sharp pain in my heart like I've never felt before. (a 6 on the scale of 1-10). "Almost" as if i 6-inch dagger was slowly inserted in my heart/chest. 5 seconds later another of the same sharp pain only increased to a 7. I was thinking in my mind "oh my God, is this it?". Just then, 5 seconds later, another! At an 8! I thought I was going to die right there at Boot Camp! So I yelled help (or whatever I said screaming out in pain). And then the 4rth and last pain hit me, again 5 seconds apart and again increasing and now it was at a 9. Truly, in my mind, I was about to die, the next one was to surely to end my life. (Convinced because of the severity of the attacks in my heart.) But the attacks stopped. I had a little trouble breathing for a while but then that went away. By the time I got in my car to head home, I was breathing fine and felt great like it never happened. (Except for 4 days of soreness and bruising like someone punched me in really hard, in the EXACT same spot at to where Paul laid just the 4 top half of 4 fingers on me for a quick prayer.)

But it did! And is was no heart attack. It was real and it was no accident. And what I discovered is that it was not a 6-inch dagger being inserted slowly into my heart. It was God pulling those 4 deep embedded hurts and resentments out by the roots. Ripping them out 1 by 1.

It was God doing for me what I could not do for myself. I woke up the next morning and spoke with all 3 of those children and set a path for amends, and invited my mother to Thanksgiving at my home.

I cannot thank Tina and Margaret enough, and all of you for being a part of healing in my life.

I will continue to pray for each and every one of you and I will continue to reach out as a friend.

No Longer Left Out!

Jeff and Nancy Blaha

After 22 years, our marriage was over. My husband had betrayed my trust and I was done. I no longer liked him let alone loved him and I saw no hope of ever getting those feelings back.

He moved out and I went to see a divorce attorney. My future as I had envisioned was gone almost overnight.

We talked little over the next month except to discuss our next steps and I would only meet him in public places one of them being our church.

One day, our pastor's wife told us about Relationship Lifeline and how it had helped others she knew with their relationship problems. One couple in particular happened to be at church that day and they shared their experience how they would not be together today had they not gone to Relationship Lifeline.

I felt that it was useless to try anything else in our case, but after some convincing, I agreed to go to their 4-day event.

At the end of the first day, through one of the exercises I was able to crack open the door to forgiving my husband and by the end of the weekend I felt myself falling back in love with this man.

I was blown away as I thought that was totally impossible. With another exercise he got what it would be like to lose me and was willing to do anything for that not to happen.

And we both were able to trace some of our own issues that we brought into the marriage that contributed to the mess we had found ourselves in. At the end of the weekend, we both were dedicated to trying to make it work. And I can honestly say that now more than 4 years later, I am more in love with this man than ever.

Thank you Relationship Lifeline for doing the seemingly impossible!

Dori

Dear Relationship Lifeline Team,

I would like to take this opportunity to express my immense gratitude to your program. I walked in to this seminar with the expectation that I would gain some professional experience and insight in my field(counseling). Instead of furthering my career what I actually gained was harmony and healing in my own life. Like most, I have struggled with pain in my life and in just 4 short days I feel that I have completely conquered the battle. This boot camp has brought a miraculous closure that cannot even really be described in words. I have been able to resolve deep issues from childhood that up until this point I thought would be something I would always carry with me. I am in awe that I was able to finally let go. Marriage Help Centers is not only for couples. One can grow as person individually as I have. Ron, Tina, Jenny and team - I cannot even begin to thank-you. In my eyes you are all messengers of God, true angels on this earth. I am now at peace with myself and look forward to living a loving and fulfilling life. Please know that I will continue spread the word to everyone I know how transformational and exceptionally special your program is.

Cara

Hi Tina,

I wanted to share with you how much this program has helped my marriage and, my relationship with my Mom who passed away a month ago. Chris and Ellie Boudreau were the ones who introduced us to Lifeline. My husband and I were separated over the summer and they shared with us how life changing this program was! It definitely brought my husband and I back together but I also came into the weekend with a lot of mixed emotions about my Mom. We had been estranged since my Dad passed away in 2009 and because of my Mom's personality and poor choices she was living in a nursing home completely alone with no friends or family. She had pushed everyone away because of her victim mentality and she was a toxic person to be around. On the night of forgiveness, I chose to forgive my Mom for not being the grandma to my kids I needed her to be and how since I was a child she had made me responsible for her all her joy, sadness and anger, disappointment, etc. I am an only child so it was a huge responsibility I felt even though my Dad was there he would just side with her.

So the biggest thing I learned through Lifeline was COMPASSION. I thought I had a ton of compassion!

I've been doing volunteer work with children and the elderly since I was 16 years old because of how much I enjoyed helping people. Well that weekend taught me to have even more especially for my husband and Mom. I did forgive my Mom that night especially when you told us to picture that person as a child. Wow, that made me see things completely different! My husband and I came through this past August and on October 23rd I got a phone call from my Mom's lawyer that she was in the hospital in ICU and not doing well at all. Now my Mom had been in the hospital a few times before this while we were estranged but I never went to see her. She had even tried to commit suicide about 2 years ago and I still did not go see her because I was done. My husband and I tried in every way possible to help my Mom financially, physically, and emotionally when my Dad passed away but she didn't want to do it our way and refused to work at it with us. We had 2 kids and a newborn at the time so our hands were full! So this time when I got the call about her being in the hospital I felt different about it because of what you, Margaret, Rocky and Rob taught me. I went straight to the hospital that night and she was in critical condition. She was of course very surprised to see me! A few days after that they told me she needed to go into hospice that there was nothing else they could do. She had 3 severe infections going on and it damaged her lungs beyond repair and there were no other options. She spent a week in the hospital and then they had to move her to a 24-hour care facility where she passed away a week later on November 7th.

What I wanted you all to know is that I got to spend 2 weeks with my Mom because of this program. I had compassion for her, we were able to tell each other how much we loved each other, we got to do simple things like watch TV together. I was with her every single day for those 2 weeks holding her hand, bugging nurses constantly to make her more comfortable, feeding her, and just sharing things with her about my kids. It was so physically and emotionally exhausting for those 2 weeks but it was such a gift to both of us. I had my Mom again even though it was only for 2 weeks. I really missed taking care of her when she died. I KNOW for a fact that without Relationship Lifeline I would have not gotten those 2 precious weeks with my Mom because of all I learned about having compassion. I can't even imagine how I would have dealt with her death if I had never been able to speak to her again. I know without a doubt that God brought Chris and Ellie into our life to repair my marriage and to give me that time with my Mom. They also visited my Mom in the hospital and Ellie helped my Mom accept Jesus as her Lord and Savior a few days before she passed. It was a truly beautiful thing to witness and I could see the change come over my Mom. As far as I'm concerned, Chris and Ellie are angels that were sent to me! I am so thankful for all the memories my Mom and I made and will always cherish them.

I was so disappointed I was not able to volunteer in November and this month because of everything going on. I have come back to help twice so far and just love it so much! I feel truly honored to be able to help this program in whatever way I can. I will FOREVER be grateful to you, your husband, Margaret, Rocky and Rob for the gifts you have given me, my husband, our 3 children and my Mom. I am so excited about the new year and hope I can help the people half as much as the TA's from my weekend helped me! Thank you!

These testimonials that you will read on our web site all have some common denominators. These individuals and couples all demonstrate a strength and courage to work hard, to go to difficult places, and to endure unbelievable pain in the "Reveal" process. They leave with clarity and direction. It is these couples and individuals that I raise my hands in praise to. They inspire us and encourage us to keep on doing what we do. This second printing is dedicated to all those who have come out the other end with new resolve and new purpose for a healthier and happier life and a living legacy for their children!

PART TWO

MONEY SECTION

CHAPTER 16

ROOT OF YOUR
MONEY BELIEFS

–Tina

It is a difficult premise to acknowledge wounds that can go back to infancy. It is hard to reconcile, hard to accept and so hard to relive and reconstruct. As we developed the Reveal, Rewrite and Renew processes, it was inevitable that we would each have to do our own inventory and as a result, look at the barriers that kept us from realizing our potentials. This applied not only to our emotional and spiritual blocks but also to our financial belief systems and practices.

When I was nine months old, I was sent from Belgium to live with my grandparents in Italy. It was years later, when I was in my early 20s, that I questioned and began to hear the stories of why.

My parents, shortly after getting married, acquired a lot of debt with a home, new furnishings and a business that they had purchased. They made the decision—that was not foreign to European families—to send me to extended family members to care for me when I was only 9 months! I had to be sent off in order for them to work long hours. Psychologically, I was too young to have any recollection of it, but emotionally I was old enough to be damaged. The damage was uncovered when I returned home nine months later.

I demonstrated such anger that my 17-year-old mother was afraid of me. I had transformed from being a loving, happy and fun baby, to an 18-month-old terror. I literally took the fire poker and went about ruining all the new dining room chairs (which were a portion of their debt) while my mom could do nothing but observe. At 18 months old, I was already destroying possessions.

There had to be a huge disconnect from the nurturing that a mother gives versus a distant family member. A surreal belief system about money began to take nurture. "Mom and Dad will come get you when they make more money," "They love you and miss you, but they don't have enough money to care for you," and so on! So at this young infant state, I had already been indoctrinated that "money and love could not abide together," and "that money takes away people that really love you".

Every person has a money belief system. It is your personal belief system, and it is unique to you. You created it for you, and therefore, you know it well. Think of your brain as a large filing cabinet in which there are many folders you can retrieve with ease. These folders are accessed when needed, usually in the realm of decision making. It is what I call your financial comfort zone.

All belief systems are made up of either:

1) truths, or 2) untruths (lies).

We all have inner programs based on the truth or the lies. I refer to these inner programs as Mind Chatter. The Mind Chatter is formed through what we heard, saw and experienced.

If you were always picked last as a child for a team, you most likely have formed the chatter that says, "Do not play team sports because your feelings will get hurt." This affects the way we think, feel and act. Consciously or subconsciously, the chatter is constantly playing in your head. The repeat button is set on "forever and ever." It is up to you to ReVeal – ReWrite and Renew.

SPECIAL NOTE: Lies become truth to you when you decide to believe them.

Let me give you a definition of Mind Chatter: Mind Chatter is an opinion formed in the "then and there" and is stored in our brain's filing cabinet for reference.

EXERCISE

Use the next page with the word "MONEY" written at the top to make a list. Start writing the first negative, toxic thoughts that come to your mind. Try not to censor or filter your thoughts, just write them out. Here are a few common examples of Mind Chatter:

Money is the root of all evil.

Money doesn't grow on trees.

Work hard for your money.

Rich people are arrogant.

I don't want to be like my parents.

Money

1. _____

_____

2. _____

_____

3. _____

_____

4. _____

_____

5. _____

_____

6. _____

_____

7. _____

_____

8. _____

_____

9. _____

_____

10. _____

_____

(If you don't think you have 10 toxic thoughts about money,
think a bit harder. Try to think of things you remember
your parents or people you look up to saying and how
it's affected your way of thinking about your finances.)

How was this Mind Chatter formed? Where did it originate from?

They originated from:

1. What you have heard

2. What you have seen

3. What you have experienced

Let's take a look at:

1. What you have heard

As a child, you heard adults refer to money in a negative and/or positive way. You heard their opinions on money, which in turn, formed your money chatter. These money thoughts are passed down from generation to generation. The exercise that you did on the previous page should help you begin to identify those messages. You have adopted those messages from previous generations as truth. The chatter that was adopted as truths then began to form who you were personally and in your relationships. The reason for going down memory lane is this: more often than not, this same chatter is still telling you what to do today even if it's not working for you.

2. What you have seen

What we saw as children also holds great bearing on our attitudes toward money today. If what we saw was fighting as a result of money (which was my experience), or struggling and sadness, then we are bound to feel the emotional repercussions. This can lead us to anger, sadness, broken relationships or even defeat in our financial realm.

3. What you have experienced

Our experiences are what really give our chatter validity and make them stick. Something happens, you experience it, and it becomes a part of your thoughts, which then becomes a part of your emotions. This is what formed your Mind Chatter.

When I was in grade seven, my father left to work out of town. Can you guess why? If you guessed debts, then you are right. This came as no surprise to me, seeing as how my chatter was well instilled by now. "Money takes love away." That was my truth!

While my father was away, my grade seven class had planned a trip to Victoria, BC, Canada for the day. This was to celebrate our graduation from elementary school to high school. I couldn't go. I was the only child who was unable to participate. Our family couldn't afford it.

There were other families that couldn't afford it either yet their kids were going. But there was a rule in our family: "You don't share your dirty laundry with others." What did that mean in my situation? It meant that when the school offered to pay my way, the offer was turned down because that was unacceptable. That would have been too great an embarrassment to my mother and father to accept such charity.

I experienced extreme anger and sadness that day and in the weeks following, especially when the other children spoke of the trip. My negative money chatter had been re-affirmed, and more negative thoughts were formed.

Both negative and positive chatter controls your finances, and ultimately, this chatter can run your life. It is, therefore, important for us to identify these inner programs. You cannot change the lies that you have believed if you do not first ReVeal them. The truth needs to be part of your ReWrite of the lies, and you must commit to ReNew the truth daily so that your inner belief system is based on truth.

I believe that our Mind Chatter has set a course for our life. Ron and I had been working in the field of personal development since 1980. As we worked with children and youth, it was evident how much effect their circumstances had on their self-esteem and self-worth. We could watch belief systems being built in their minds and hearts. As young impressionable youths, it was easy to implant both negative and positive thoughts.

In the years following, we began to develop programs to help youths and adults recognize the power of the concept that "what you believe will be your truth."

It has often been said that we create what we fear. In other words, when we fear something, we are constantly thinking about it (whether we realize it or not) and eventually, we bring it onto ourselves. For example, how many people do you know who said "I'll never be like my mother/father," and they end up being an exact replica of their parent? Or we fear being broke. So what happens? The larger and more intense we allow that fear to take hold, the more broke we get. We lose our job, our stocks go down, we get swindled, etc... Can you relate?

The Story about Investment

"It's also like a man going off on an extended trip. He called his servants together and delegated responsibilities. To one he gave five thousand dollars, to another he gave two thousand dollars, to a third one thousand, depending on their abilities. Then he left. Right off, the first servant went to work and doubled his master's investment. The second did the same. But the man with the single thousand dug a hole and carefully buried his master's money.

"After a long absence, the master of those three servants came back and settled up with them. The one given five thousand dollars showed him how he had doubled his investment. His master commended him: 'Good work! You did your job well. From now on be my partner.'

"The servant with the two thousand dollars showed him he had doubled his master's investment. His master commended him: 'Good work! You did your job well. From now on be my partner.'

"The servant given one thousand said, 'Master, I know you have high standards and hate careless ways, that you demand the best and make no allowances for error. I was afraid I might disappoint you, so I found a good hiding place and secured your money. Here it is, safe and sound down to the last cent.'

"The master was furious. 'That's a terrible way to live! It's criminal to live cautiously like that! If you knew I was after the best, why did you do less than the least? The least you could have done would have been to invest the sum with the bankers, where at least I would have gotten a little interest.'

> *"Take the thousand and give it to the one who risked the most..."* *(Matthew 25:14-28, The Message/Remix by Eugene H. Peterson)*

This is where you need to wake up and smell the coffee.

The point of the story is that to everyone who has a belief of abundance, whatever they have will multiply. For the person who has a belief of scarcity or fear of loss, even what they have will be taken.

CONCLUSION

Our money experience has been formed by our belief system. This belief system is our "here and now," better known as our "reality."

Dear Reader, this is worth repeating: "You cannot change what you do not ReVeal first." — ReVeal

Identify and acknowledge the lies which have become truths to you. You can't fool your inner belief system. Any thought which is repeated will be acted on and adopted as truth. — ReWrite

Begin to replace them with real, positive truths. — ReNew

"Act as if everything you think, say and do determines your entire life — because in reality, it does." — Laurel Adrian, author

CHAPTER 17

FINANCIAL SUICIDE POOR MONEY MANAGEMENT

–Tina

Money management was never my strong suit. I knew how to make a lot of money but because of my money programming, I was always more successful at losing it. My comfort zone was to "make it and lose it."

When my father passed away, he left a sizeable inheritance to me. The one thing I was sure of was that it was not my money, so I could not treat it the same way I had treated mine. I would not allow myself to leverage that inheritance to support one more investment, which would ultimately fail. So that money was safe, or so I thought.

You see, even if you set new goals, when your money programming (belief system) doesn't change, there is still your go to or default system in control. You attract that which you fear. I still had the primal fear that "money and love cannot abide together." This causes things to happen outside your control. So what happened to my inheritance?

Three years after my father's passing, Ron and I were audited because of our new net worth. I didn't take it too seriously. I knew inheritance dollars are non-taxable, so I believed I could clear the whole matter up without breaking a sweat. Well, it wasn't that easy, you see. Because of poor money management, I hadn't reported my inheritance.

I learned very quickly that nothing is easy with Revenue Canada. In less than three months of looking at my very messy books, they believed that I owed them $1,000,000. Yes, you saw it right—one million dollars!

My belief system made sure that I did not have a good money management system in place. If I had had a good one, then the money I made would multiply, and I would lose my family, just like when I was a child. My comfort zone, remember, was to "make it and lose it."

My brain tried to fool my belief system by saying, "This is not your money; it is your father's hard earned money." Obviously, it didn't work. Your outer results are, more often than not, telling you what is going on in the inside.

There was a movie that came out years ago that coined the phrase "it just doesn't matter." John Bellushi, the main actor in the movie, was expressing that even if they won all the summer camp Olympics, they still wouldn't get the girls from the rich camp. He said: "it just doesn't matter."

My point is "it just doesn't matter" how much money you make. If your inner belief system is flawed and you don't manage your money well, chances are you may still be broke or in the least, not have the freedom your finances should give you. Your belief system is what matters. So change your inner belief system, and make your freedom matter.

There are people who manage to live, save, invest and have money for fun left over on an income of $35,000 per year. They have a belief system that money properly managed will produce good results. On the other hand, there are individuals who earn in excess of $100,000 and yet live from paycheck to paycheck. They don't seem to be big time spenders, but their belief system is such that **you spend what you earn**.

I personally remember our family living very comfortably on much less income. When we developed a greater income flow, I did not think we lived differently but somehow at the end of the month, we didn't have the difference of cash sitting in the bank. I can imagine some of you smiling right now because you can relate.

If your inner programming is flawed and you don't know how to manage your money, financial freedom is not on your horizon yet.

Financial suicide is not about how much money you make. It is about your inner programming and your money management skills. The skills can be learned, unlike the inner programming. The inner programming needs to be mentally, emotionally and spiritually dealt with.

The inside work that needs to be done is a little more of a process. The journey that started in childhood, with the negative things you heard, saw and experienced, need to be revealed and then rewritten.

You are in charge of your thoughts and you create the thoughts which create the circumstances in your life. Do not underestimate the power of your thoughts. The circumstances in your life are not an accident. — ReVeal

"...for the thief comes only to steal, kill and destroy." — John 10:10

Negative Mind Chatter controls your financial, emotional, mental, and spiritual life. This pattern of negative thinking has the potential to act like a thief. — ReWrite & ReNew

Start by making *a decision* to take control of your thought life. If you are frustrated with your financial, emotional, mental or spiritual state, don't be afraid to get help. You can change your circumstances when you decide you want to.

p.s. In reference to the million dollars that we owed Revenue Canada, I do have one awesome thing going for me and that is my faith. I knew that cleaning up this mess was going to take a miracle, and that I could handle it, because I believe in miracles! I thank God that He provided the people I needed to help me out of that mess. The auditor, who was originally assigned to our case, went on maternity leave. This was a good thing for a lot of reasons, and it was the first of a long string of miracles.

Our biggest miracle came when I asked God to send someone to me who would be able to find favor in the eyes of Revenue Canada. That "someone" turned out to be Vince, an acquaintance of ours who is a financial consultant. I didn't go looking for him; we were simply having a conversation about his opting to not own a car at this stage in his life. This ordinary conversation was the beginning of the extraordinary saving grace which saved us from our potential financial suicide. Not only did Vince offer to review our books, but he told us not to worry about the cost. I cannot even estimate how many hours and sleepless nights he spent toiling over our BIG MESS—our $1,000,000 mess, to be precise. Over the course of one year, he worked without asking for so much as a dime. He was not only reviewing our books, but he was having meetings with supervisors and auditors at Revenue Canada. Agents at Revenue Canada began to help us make sense out of the chaos which my poor money management had created.

I believe my faith in this circumstance rose above what could have been financial ruin. God took a mess and made it a message. A message that is loud and clear in this book. It is a message of hope, hope that our past miss-management of finances and our negative belief system can change. It is now my responsibility to practice my new belief system and money management skills.

I am thankful today for my friend Vince.

Let's get back to our financial programming. If you are not in full control of your financial destiny, ask yourself, "Why not?" What fears are paralyzing you from financially living at your full potential?

The sooner you ReVeal these fears, the sooner you can begin the journey of financial success. You can create wealth when, and only when, you have a healthy heart toward money. You won't allow yourself to have money if you fear money or success.

Fear can sometimes be a positive thing. It is programmed into us for a reason. It helps us to consciously think about things before we do them. But when the fear controls us and causes our Mind Chatter to mistrust, it stunts our growth.

"We can learn for instance that sticking our finger in a flame of fire will hurt, without being forever afraid of fire. It is about action and consequence, not fear and mistrust. We can know from experience that if we stick our finger in the flame we will get burnt, but we then don't necessarily have to put out every flame we see." — Suze and Otto Collins, relationship coaches.

For me, how could I possibly attract wealth (even though I strived so hard to attain it) if my Mind Chatter was telling me that I would lose my loved ones? I was programmed to lose money so that I could keep my family. When I finally evicted that fear, I gave my destiny permission to proceed and become all that God had purposed me to be financially.

I feared the loss of my husband and children if I allowed myself to become wealthy. So my fear-based faith worked hard at not allowing wealth to abide in our home.

If you do not have a proper money management system in place, could it be that it is not because you don't have time, but because it's of your fear of money?

Suze Orman, in her book, *The 9 Steps to Financial Freedom*, states, *"The mind gives us thousands of ways to say no, but there's only one way to say yes, and that's from the heart."*

"Successful people make a habit of doing the things they fear." — Brian Tracey

CHAPTER 18

YOUR BELIEFS ARE YOUR DRIVING FORCE

–Tina

As I have already shared, my chatter about money began at a very early age. In my family, money controlled over 90% of what went on in our home. Money could even control God in my eyes. I learned that nearly every decision was made by money. Where we lived, what job we had, what business we did, what we owned, what we didn't own and what we wore. The list went on.

My biggest belief about money was, "money equals loss." Loss of home, loss of country, loss of parents, loss of grandparents, loss of friends, loss of schools, loss of happiness, loss of love, loss of church, and loss of happy times. In my mind, there was nothing that money didn't take away.

The good news in all of this is:

Knowledge is power – when we ReVeal our inner programming, then we are in a position of power. Now to tap into the power of knowledge, we must make a decision to take action. In other words, knowledge without action is like power in reserve. It just sits there. But if we want to achieve a positive driving force in our finances and all other areas of our life, we must put together:

KNOWLEDGE + ACTION

When we put those two together, here's what happens:

KNOWLEDGE + ACTION = RESULTS

How can you tell what your money programming is? It is really simple, just look at your results. Are you happy with your results?

If you want to really change your results, it's an absolute must that you change your negative expectations and learn to expect the best for you. It is imperative that you break the cycle of negative and toxic thinking at the heart level.

On a daily basis, we give away positive and negative gifts. I refer to them as gifts because it is what we so freely give, to our children, spouse, family, friends, and co-workers. We are all destined to leave a legacy. What do you want your legacy to look like?

Let's examine, for a moment, the gifts that we give away every day. On the negative side, we give away such things as anger, frustration, resentment, and gossip. The gift list could go on.

Challenge yourself to give such gifts as faith, love, hope, joy, optimism, good ethics, generosity, patience and more. Remind yourself of the Golden Rule: treat others the way you want to be treated.

You can become the best *you* ever. It takes effort and willingness to reverse the toxic cycle. Living at your best is living a faith-based life, on purpose. Jesus said, *"According to your faith, let it be unto you." Matt. 9:29*

ReVeal

It is a sad truth, but you cannot give what you do not have. Our circumstances, negative or positive, are a result of our faith, beliefs, and fears.

ReWrite and ReNew

If you really want to change your present financial circumstances, then you must make a decision to change your beliefs and expectations in your money programming.

CHAPTER 19

COUNT THE COST

–Tina

The lies I believed about money have cost me millions of dollars and countless hours of happiness. I can say that with confidence, based on how many times fear has led me to sell great investments.

One time in particular, our family invested in a city lot, which was bound to rise in price. My belief system sabotaged the success immediately. We proceeded to sell because we were afraid of getting stuck with it. A short six months later, the same lot was sold for over $200,000 more than what we had sold it for. Unfortunately, there are too many stories which are reminiscent of that one.

When I count the cost of the lies and the fear, I give myself permission to be angry and take back what I have lost.

My life has taken a phenomenal, 360-degree turn. The reason I can confess that is because I began the journey of replacing my lies with the truth. The lie that controlled my life was buried deep within me. It was not enough to acknowledge that money meant loss, but even deeper than that, it was my fundamental belief that if I had money, I would become like my mother. I did not want to be like my mother. So, in my twisted way of thinking, if I didn't have money, then I would not have to worry about being like my mom.

I'm not sure which lies have been in control of your finances. I'm not sure what those lies have cost you. But if you are like most people going through life simply enduring it, STOP NOW. I cannot speak for you, but I did not want to continue complaining and not do anything about it.

Joyce Meyer says, *"Complain and remain."* I was sick and tired of losing my hard-earned money through the holes in my pockets. I was past due in dealing with my belief system.

When you are sick and tired of what your belief system has done to your finances, then you are ready for change. Be encouraged. Change from a negative mindset to a positive one has awesome rewards.

If you are living without joy because of your finances, reach out for help. If your relationships are in trouble because of your finances, reach out for help. Financial challenges are not life threatening; at least, they should not be.

How much has your money programming stolen from you? Has it stolen your peace? Has it stolen your freedom? Maybe even your health or sanity? What about time with your loved ones? Statistics say that the number one reason for marriage breakups is caused by money issues. Debt and not having enough money left over at the end of the month is a major cause of stress. Many physical illnesses are due to financial stress.

If you are caught up in making excuses (and no excuse is valid if it is an excuse), make a decision to be responsible. Excuses make you helpless. Excuses are for victims. There is no power in being a victim. Victims do not move ahead. Victims live in the past. No one is denying that you and I, at some time or another, were victims of our circumstances and our lies. But you now have the power of *decision* to bring it to a halt.

For years, I blamed my mother for my failures and lack of success. It was not until I was prepared to stop playing the blame game that I became free to succeed. I was not only free to succeed in my finances, but in other areas of my life as well. It began with my parenting skills. My upbringing was not always an example of a loving way to raise children. When my daughter was 10 years old, I decided to stop the unhealthy cycle. So I made a change. I discovered that certain areas of my life were flawed by my belief system. I made a conscious decision to take full responsibility for my own failures. I counted the cost of the lies, which I had packed around for so long, and I made truth my friend. The truth, once it was applied, had the power to set me free. Free to be the loving parent my daughter deserved.

The first step to improving your financial future is to ReVeal your situation. Then take action by rewriting and renewing your future and watch as the results spring out of nowhere (or so it may seem).

ReVeal

If you are not willing to take full responsibility for where you are at today, your financial situation will not change. Admit with all sincerity that, maybe, you haven't made the wisest decisions and choices and too much has been lost, but you are willing to embrace the truth today.

ReWrite and ReNew

If you are serious about moving on with your life, make the decision that the lies will no longer be in control and put truth in the driver's seat.

CHAPTER 20

ARE YOU READY AND WILLING?

–Tina

When I was finally ready to face the truth, I became willing to put a stop to the madness. Every time I think of the opportunities presented to me in real estate where fear continuously prevailed, hindering me from taking the leap, I get angry at the lies.

My money journey really started after the passing of my father in 1998. A lot improved as far as money management was concerned but I was still operating under the old negative belief system.

Finally, I was ready and willing to receive what was best for me. It is simpler than one thinks.

It took work, but it was worth it. I was finally able to receive all that was out there which was entirely for me. It was my destiny. I deserved it. How freeing that thought was. It was not about making millions of dollars; it was about being my best and living at my full potential.

The apostle Paul said, *"Not that I have already attained, but putting the past behind and pressing toward the mark of the high calling."* Philippians 3:12

What does that mean? It means that his destiny was ahead of him and he had to press toward his purpose and leave his past failures behind.

How many times have you prevented something good from happening to you because you didn't believe that it was meant for you? Maybe your belief system isn't in conjunction with all that is out there for you. Being ready and believing that you can succeed go hand in hand.

An Olympian would not prepare for his/her event if he/she did not believe that they had the ability to win. If you do not believe that you can succeed, then why would you put all of the effort into it? We all believe that we aspire to win in our finances, in our happiness, in our relationships, and in our careers, but our self-image (again controlled by our belief system) limits us in how far we can go. Your self-image is not based on how others see you, but on how you value yourself. If you perceive yourself as a loser, then you would not even enroll yourself in the game of winning.

The truth is that most people are only willing to prepare for success if they honestly and truly believe that they are able to have it. Most people are afraid of failure. This fear often leads to the "Why bother trying?" mentality. Are you starting to see how you attract what you fear? You must be ready and willing to prepare yourself for success. You cannot attract anything of more value than the value that you give to yourself.

Do you believe that success is a result of luck? If that is what your belief system tells you, then you are not ready for this awesome change. How many times have you heard it said, "He was in the right place at the right time"? What a misconception. The chances of being successful due to luck are the same as the chances of winning the lottery. Success comes to those who are prepared, ready and willing to do the inner work first, then follow a practical and, preferably, simple plan.

When you become successful, you may not appreciate someone thinking you were just lucky. They would not be recognizing the work you have been willing to do to achieve your success. Like the Olympian, you must appreciate that they have not just shown up at the Olympics and gotten lucky. They have put in the time and effort. It pays off, and they are successful.

The desire to succeed is important, but the willingness to prepare is equally significant.

ReVeal

Ask yourself if you are afraid of failure or success and why?

ReWrite....

Your belief that success is only for the "lucky and the strong." Start by believing *you* can be successful and *you* can take the necessary steps to reach your full financial potential.

ReNew

You get to make the decision to live on purpose. Life is too short to miss out on any more opportunities.

NOW WHAT?

In 1995, I was challenged by something that Rev. Robert Schuler said: "If failure was not an option and money was not an obstacle, what would you be doing with your life?"

Wow! That was such a powerful question for me. That single question empowered and motivated me to get a vision which had no limits.

Fear had me tormented into believing "I can't do it" and "I can't afford it." This negative mindset had me paralyzed in a dormant, dead vision. I had the vision; I just didn't have the faith to drive the vision. I was in a prison of self-doubt. I believed the lies that told me: "This is too hard," and "I don't have what it takes to make it big."

I had to overcome those lies and replace them with truth. If I had listened to them, I would not be doing what I love and living out my purpose. I would be living in a box created by my Mind Chatter. I decided that fear would not control my life anymore and in order to be successful, I would have to follow my vision with full force.

Begin the journey of having a vision by asking yourself, "What do I want in my life?" Take a moment now to really think about what you want in your life. You may have to think back to when you were a kid or when you were in college or maybe just recently. But at some point, you have compromised your dreams and visions.

What did you want before your dreams became tainted by debt, bills, work, stress, fear and life in general? Make a list, devoid of fear and lies, of what you really want in life. Do not be afraid of sounding selfish or silly or extreme. This list is for YOU to realize your dreams.

Most people do not have what they want, because they don't know what they want. (Don't forget Rev. Schuler's powerful statement "If failure is not an option and money is not an obstacle.")

What I Want

1. _____

_____

_____

_____

2. _____

_____

_____

_____

3. _____

_____

_____

_____

4. _____

_____

_____

_____

5. _____

_____

_____

_____

Go over your list until you truly understand what you want your life to mean. Going about getting what you want is a simple concept, it's just not easy. It is not easy because every day your inner programming, which has been built by your belief system over the years, is not willing to let you simply push the delete button. It is fighting back. It is forcing you to decide what to do with the negative mindset that is already a part of your comfort zone.

It is near impossible that you or I can reach our full potential in any area of our lives with a mind full of negative/toxic thoughts and a heart full of negative/toxic feelings. Thoughts and feelings of fear, worry, scarcity and failure.

ReVeal

If you keep telling yourself, "Oh, this is just too much or too hard for me," then admit it and let's move on to healing by rewriting this lie.

ReWrite and ReNew

Give yourself permission to have a vision. Write your vision, and then be willing to do what it takes to make it happen.

CHAPTER 21

DARE TO DREAM

"I have had a lot of dreams, some have come true, some have not, but I'm glad I had them."

— Author unknown

–Tina

People are meant to have dreams. When the desire to dream is lost, life becomes dull.

I remember a time when it was too painful to dream. My dream had nearly cost me my family. I was scared. A new belief was created: "Dreams are not safe." It took a long time before I allowed myself to remember that life without dreams is not life at all.

If you are scared, think of the alternative. Your financial, relationship, and spiritual success depends on your willingness to dream.

Eleanor Roosevelt said it best: "The future is in the power of our dreams."

There is no time like the present to go for it. Dare to dream. We say "dare" because it can be scary. You don't have to be dared to do something that you are not afraid of, you'll just do it. But we have to realize that it doesn't take any more effort to believe in positive dreams than to believe in negative ones. Do not let the fear to dream control your future. You "get to dream."

Don't use your past failures as an excuse to not act on your future.

Each one of us has the power to do things that we never dreamed possible. This power can be tapped into, simply by our willingness to change our negative core beliefs, thus eliminating the limitations which we have put onto ourselves by our negative Mind Chatter.

DARE TO DREAM… hang out with dreamers.

ReVeal

Take inventory of your surroundings. The best way to change your thoughts is by changing your surroundings. If your friends are negative and fearful, then spend less time with them and more time with people who are positive and bold. The popular idea that you are defined by the company you keep has some truth in it. Many people tend to drag you down because they are afraid of being left behind. In most cases, gravity wins. You will be dragged down before you can pull them up.

ReWrite

Develop relationships that will help you reach your goals and your dreams. You can choose your friends. It is important that those closest to you want you to succeed.

ReNew

Let this be your motto:

"Whatever things are true, whatever things are honest, whatever things are just, whatever things are pure, whatever things are lovely, whatever things are of good report; if there is

any virtue, and if there is any praise, think on these things."
Philippians 4:8

Does that mean that you drop all of your negative friends? No. First, give them the opportunity to take the journey of growth with you. If your friends are willing to work hard and take the journey from the head to the heart, then do it together. If they are not, they have made a decision to stay in their negative state. Choose to move on. You can still love them and hope that one day they will see your positive growth and want the same for themselves. But guard yourself. Always be aware of the gifts that people are trying to give to you. Remember, it is your decision to accept or reject a negative gift. There is a reason that you don't generally see successful people having intimate relationships with those unwilling to change.

William Backus & Marie Chapian, authors of *TruthTalk,* describe love this way: *"Love means acting in the other person's best interests. If I love you, I speak the truth to you, not only for my benefit, but for yours."*

CHAPTER 22

WHO IS IN CONTROL?

It has often been said that either you control your money or it controls you. I examined my own life and found that money really was in control. Though I did not want to re-create my childhood experience, it seemed that I had done just that.

There was a time when my marriage was in an emotional upheaval, money was a harsh concern. In our attempt to keep life normal, for the children's sake, we thought it best not to concern them. I remember I had been invited to go to Portland, Oregon to speak at a seminar. The evening before the seminar commenced, my husband and I lay in bed in our hotel room. As I lay there I began to cry, under the assumption that the children were asleep. I began sharing my concern with my husband. "With this mess that we are in, what are we going to do about money"? The conversation went on for a while, my husband desperately trying to console me. I was terrified about our financial situation.

Suddenly, my 12-year-old son was standing at my bedside, and with a most sincere voice, offered his contribution: "Mom, I have a hundred dollars that you can have." My heart shattered into a million little pieces at that moment, realizing that I had just instilled my fear into my son.

The fear of scarcity was alive and well in our home. When your mentality is one of scarcity, then money is in control.

It is not always necessary to get rid of the fear first. Recognize the truth first and, because we are creatures of habit, begin to act in spite of the fear. Take control. Don't let fear, self-doubt and negative Mind Chatter continue to control your success and happiness.

Your fear factor does not have to be negative. It can be your springboard into action. Your goal is to overcome fear, not by ignoring it, but by taking action. Successful people act in spite of fear, whereas victims act in consensus with fear.

Begin to build a new relationship with money. This time, you can consciously make it a healthy relationship which consists of healthy principles. Set goals around your vision. Write them down and be specific. Believe it or not, writing is power. Fear can read.

There is a children's song entitled *"Practice Makes Perfect."* Practice being in control and watch the fear dissipate. Focus on changing what you can control: *yourself.*

Fear tries to prevent you from taking action. It is imperative you realize that even the most successful people have fear and doubt. The difference between them and victims of fear is their action. Successful people don't let these feelings stop them. It may not be possible to rid yourself of the fear and doubt completely, but it is possible to control the effect they have on you.

I urge you to work hard at taking control of your future and not allow yesterday's failures to determine your tomorrow.

CONCLUSION

Do not let fear, self-doubt and negative, toxic Mind Chatter continue to control your financial, relational and spiritual success.

SOLUTION

Focus on what you can change: yourself.

Don't be afraid to reach out for help. If you have resisted the truth, based on your results, make today the day for change. Go one step beyond reading this book (like so many other books you have read and not applied) and visit my website www.tinakonkin.com and join the thousands who have begun the journey of healing.

The benefits of this intensive seminar:

- How your childhood tapes (opinions adopted as truth) affect you today
- The inner programming of your money belief system
- Why knowledge alone does not create abundance
- How you can trade the lies you have believed into life-changing truth

- How to RESET your belief system for success
- How to train your "mind" to reverse the negative cycle

And that's just the beginning...

Are you ready to

ReVeal

ReWrite

ReNew

and let it set you free?

ENDNOTES

Chapter 2

[1] http://www.thefreedictionary.com/love

Chapter 4

[2] Note: Dr Phil McGraw's partner facilitated the program my husband and I attended and it is because of our personal healing that we do what we do today. We are beyond passionate when it comes to healing the broken hearted. The programs we facilitate are a resource for Dr. Phil and many other churches and organizations throughout the world. We are also a resource for therapists and attorneys.

Please visit www.relationshiplifeline.org for more information on programs offered by Relationship Lifeline or call 800.718.4650.

To book Tina Konkin as a conference speaker, visit www.TinaKonin.com.

Chapter 9

[3] Author: Glen Rein, PhD , Rollin McCraty, PhD Institute of HeartMath; Date: 01/01/2001